Lessons from JOSEPH

A Journey from Dreams to Destiny

Andrew Wommack

Published in partnership between Andrew Wommack Ministries and Harrison House Publishers.

Woodland Park, CO 80863 – Shippensburg, PA 17257

ISBN 13 TP: 978-1-66750-427-8

For Worldwide Distribution, Printed in the USA

1 2 3 4 5 6 / 26 25 24

Contents

Introduction

Now all these things happened unto them for examples: and they are written for our admonition, upon whom the ends of the world are come.

1 Corinthians 10:11

Everything that happened to people in the Old Testament was written so that we might learn from them. The experiences of these people are how I've learned a lot of things that helped me in my life and ministry.

In general, your life is a sum total of the choices you've made. And in this book, I'm going to be talking about the life of Joseph; he certainly had things happen to him that were not a direct result of his choices. His brothers sold him into slavery (Gen. 37:28). His master accused him of committing adultery with his wife and put him into prison (Gen. 39:19–20). He did have a choice, however, of how he would respond.

Joseph is a great example of someone who just went through terrible things that were completely contrary to everything that God had shown him, and yet he remained faithful.

There were things that happened to Joseph that were not of his choosing—that he didn't directly cause to come to pass. I believe that same thing is true of us. We live in a fallen world and there are bad things that happen to good people. But the way you react to these bad things and the choices that you make determine your outcome.

You can learn from your own experience and things that come your way, but you don't have to. I often tell people it's obvious that we learn through the school of hard knocks, but there's a better way; instead, you can learn from other people's examples, the teachers in your life, and by reading the stories of people in the Bible.

Most people have not seen these truths in the life of Joseph. And most people don't make a practical application to their life from what was written about Joseph. This isn't just a story about what happened 4,000 years ago. We need to see how it relates to us. There are so many parallels between what happened with Joseph, the way that God works in our life, and how the devil comes against us.

Like Joseph, we have a choice whether we become bitter or better. We can choose to keep a good attitude and trust God. This is one of the things about Joseph that God has used to speak to me. Joseph is one of my favorite characters in the whole Bible, and I've learned lessons from his life that have blessed me. I believe they will bless you too.

Chapter 1

God Speaks Through Dreams

My understanding from Scripture is that there are only three major characters in the Old Testament who were not rebuked: Joseph, Samuel, and Daniel.

Moses killed a man, thinking it was God's will (Ex. 2:12). He got angry and did things against God's will, and because of that, the Lord wouldn't let him go into the Promised Land (Num. 20:12; Deut. 34:4). Elijah called down fire from heaven (1 Kgs. 18:36–38) and did great things, but he got so caught up in pride that he ran from Jezebel and asked God to kill him (1 Kgs. 19:2–4); so God took the ministry away from him and gave it to Elisha (2 Kgs. 2:11–13). David was a man after God's own heart (1 Sam. 13:14), but he committed adultery with Bathsheba (2 Sam. 11:1–5) and murdered Uriah to cover it up (2 Sam. 11:15, 24, 26).

In the New Testament, Paul had some major problems too. Among other things, he (as Saul) consented to the stoning death of Stephen—the first Christian martyr (Acts 7:58–60 and 8:1). Peter, of course, was always saying or doing something wrong. Sometimes, it seemed like the only time Peter opened his mouth was to change feet!

The Bible does not whitewash these characters at all. It presents them with all their warts and shows their failures along with their successes. And there are things that we can learn from them.

You can see throughout Scripture that God used and blessed imperfect people. It shows the grace of God at work, and there are great lessons to learn. Now, I'm not saying that Joseph was perfect. Nobody's perfect. But Joseph is one of only three people in the Old Testament I can think of who did not have anything negative revealed about them.

Some people are going to disagree with that and say, "Well, Joseph was a spoiled brat, and he promoted himself above his brethren. It was his arrogance that got him in trouble and caused all those bad things to happen." Some people also believe that when Joseph's brothers came into Egypt, he treated them badly because he was getting even with them (Gen. 42:6–9). But all of that is inconsistent with what the Word of God teaches.

The Bible says in Proverbs 16:18 that *"Pride goeth before destruction, and an haughty spirit before a fall."* It also says in 1 Peter 5:5 that *"God resisteth the proud, and giveth grace to the humble."* If Joseph would've been the proud, spoiled, and arrogant child a lot of people have accused him of being, I guarantee you, he never would have seen the blessings and promotions we read about in Scripture.

Now, I think the reason some people have come up with those things is because they judge Joseph by what they would have done if they'd been in a similar situation. They just impose their own personality on him. But the Bible doesn't teach this. As a matter of fact, the Bible teaches that Joseph humbled himself. The scriptural account shows him as a faithful person from the time he was a young person into adulthood.

Learn from Examples

I believe you can take the things God's Word says about Joseph and apply them to your own life. But there are a lot of people who don't think that way when they study the Bible. They read the account of Joseph's life and say, "I'm struggling to make ends meet. I'm trying to get relationships to work. What does something that happened to somebody thousands of years ago have to do with me?"

Well, the apostle Paul wrote that everything recorded in the Old Testament is there for our benefit so that we would learn what to do and what not to do (1 Cor. 10:11). And I believe we can learn a lot from the life of Joseph. His example should show us what it means to be humble in the sight of the Lord and be faithful even though our circumstances may not look like what we think they should.

I got born again when I was eight years old. I've never said a word of profanity. I've never taken a drink of liquor. I've never smoked a cigarette. I have lived a holy life. I'm not saying any of this to pat myself on the back because none of it earns me anything with God. Romans 3:23 says, *"For all have sinned, and come short of the glory of God."* I don't want to be the best sinner that ever went to hell. I had to get saved just like anybody else.

But I am saying that the reason I haven't gone into adultery, drug addiction, or any of those other things is because I have studied the Word of God from the time that I was a child. It taught me to avoid these things. This is one of the benefits of studying these people's lives and, as a result, my life has been super blessed.

I remember reading about David when I was younger and how he was a man after God's own heart (1 Sam. 13:14). David went out and fought Goliath (1 Sam 17:3–54) and did all sorts of great things, but then he took his eyes off the Lord. He got into sin with Bathsheba (2 Sam. 11:1–5) and killed her husband Uriah (2 Sam. 11:15–26). Because of that, David's daughter Tamar was raped by his son Amnon (2 Sam. 13:1–19). Amnon was killed by another son, Absalom (2 Sam. 13:22–29). Absalom was killed by David's commander (2 Sam. 18:9–15). And Adonijah, another son, was killed after he tried to assume David's throne (1 Kgs. 2:12–25).

All of these terrible things happened because David let Satan into his life and family through sin. I remember as a very young man seeing the devastation that adultery had on David and his family. I lived vicariously through David by reading the Bible and learned not to open the door to Satan through sin. I didn't have to learn it by going through the school of hard knocks—doing it all myself.

But some people are just like a goose. They just wake up in a new world every morning; they have no recollection of history. They don't think about what has happened to other people, and they just go out and learn for themselves that being a drug addict is wrong, that being an alcoholic is wrong, or that being an adulterer is wrong.

They just indulge themselves. It's only after they've suffered all kinds of pain and suffering do they come around and say, "I shouldn't have done that!" Well, I can tell you there's a better way. You can go to the Word of God and learn from the mistakes of others.

Maybe you're wondering, *God, how do I get from where I am to where You want me to be?* In Genesis 41, Joseph went from the pit to the palace in less than twenty-four hours, but there was a thirteen-year incubation period before that transformation happened. And there are things we can learn through Joseph's experience that would change your life and save you a lot of suffering. It may actually be the answer to your prayers if you are willing to receive it.

The Power of Dreams

The story of Joseph really begins with a pair of dreams. Understanding these dreams is going to be very important in understanding the story of Joseph.

> *And Joseph dreamed a dream, and he told it his brethren: and they hated him yet the more. And he said unto them, Hear, I pray you, this dream which I have dreamed: for, behold, we were binding sheaves in the field, and, lo, my sheaf arose, and also stood upright; and, behold, your sheaves stood round about, and made obeisance to my sheaf. And his brethren said to him, Shalt thou indeed reign over us? or shalt thou indeed have dominion over us? And they hated him yet the more for his dreams, and for his words. And he dreamed yet another dream, and told it his brethren, and said, Behold, I have dreamed a dream more; and, behold, the sun and the moon and the eleven stars made obeisance to me.*

> Genesis 37:5–9

God speaks through dreams. It's a biblical thing. There are fifteen instances of God speaking by dreams in the Old Testament. A number of these occurred in the story of Joseph: twice to Joseph himself (Gen. 37:5, 9), twice to Pharaoh (Gen. 41:1–8), and once each to Pharaoh's chief butler and chief baker (Gen. 40:9, 16).

Some people don't put any importance on dreams at all, but God speaks to me through dreams. I hear from Him in dreams all of the time. It would be unusual to go a week without God revealing something to me in dreams.

I'm what they call a lucid dreamer. When I dream, I sometimes can't tell whether I'm asleep or whether I'm awake. That's because my brain is working while I'm asleep just as much as it is when I'm awake. The only way I can tell that it's a dream and not me just thinking is when I start experiencing things that are totally outside of reality, like running in sand and not being able to get anywhere.

I once had a dream where I was one of Jesus' disciples. It was so vivid, I thought it was real. I saw Him raise the dead and give sight to the blind. It was awesome! I was just rejoicing with the other disciples over all the things we had seen and heard. Then Jesus whirled around, stuck his finger in my face, and asked, "But who do you say I am?"

Although I had seen Jesus do all these miraculous things in this dream, when I looked straight into the face of His humanity, it took all the faith I could muster to say, *"You are the Christ, the Son of the living God"* (Matt. 16:16 NKJV). Because that dream was so realistic, I had a better understanding of what the disciples went through as they followed Jesus. I also understood why we are blessed to see Jesus through the Scriptures with the witness of the indwelling Holy Spirit.

Not every dream I have is from God, but He speaks to me often in dreams. I'll have dreams where a person I haven't seen in years comes to mind, and in the dream, I'll pray for them. God shows me that they need ministry. When that happens, I get up and try to contact them.

Dreams can be words from God. He spoke to Daniel through dreams. God also spoke to King Nebuchadnezzar through dreams. Daniel 2:1 says,

And in the second year of the reign of Nebuchadnezzar Nebuchadnezzar dreamed dreams, wherewith his spirit was troubled, and his sleep brake from him.

When Nebuchadnezzar rose, he knew it was important. He couldn't remember what the dream was, but he knew God was speaking to him through it.

A similar thing happened to Joseph, Mary's betrothed husband, before Jesus was born. God spoke to him (Matt. 1:18–21) about the birth of Jesus and later about how they were supposed to flee into Egypt (Matt. 2:13).

The same thing happened to Pharaoh right here in Joseph's story, but we'll be dealing with that later.

Recognize Significance

I'm not saying that every dream is from God. Sometimes, a dream can come from last night's pizza because it seems so ridiculous.

I remember having a dream back when we were really struggling financially. In the dream, I quit the ministry and joined the Air Force to pay off all our debts. It's not something I would do in the natural, but this dream just seemed so real that I was actually relieved when I woke up. I lay there in bed thinking, *That was just a dream. Thank You, Jesus, that I didn't join the Air Force!* But Jamie was right there and said, "It wasn't so bad that you had to go join the Air Force." My heart started pounding as I thought, *Oh, God! It wasn't a dream!* I found out later that I had been talking in my sleep. Jamie heard the whole thing, and she decided to have some fun with it.

But God does speak through dreams. When that happens, you will just know in your heart that it is significant—that it has something to it.

These dreams Joseph had were very significant. I believe they set a course for him. God gave Joseph a purpose for his life and told him he was going to be exalted so that even his family members would come and bow down to him. That set a course for his life. These dreams were God speaking to him.

9

God was going to put him in a high position of authority, and Joseph held on to that word.

Remember as we go through this story, Joseph is not just a boy who had two dreams and happened to share them with his family before he got into all sorts of trouble. Those dreams made a huge impact on his life. And I believe those dreams kept him.

One of the things I've learned is that before God sends you on a journey, He will reveal to you something about that journey. He will prepare you for the problems and the things that you're going to face along the way.

When the Lord touched my life on March 23, 1968, by the next morning I knew that I was going to minister to people all over the world. Now, I had no clue about *how* that would happen, but it was like God just showed me something that was going to happen. All these years later, I've seen God do amazing things in my life and ministry. It's been awesome! God showed me where I was headed all the way back in 1968. I didn't know any of the details. I didn't know how I would get there. I didn't know a lot of things! But He put a dream in my heart. And I believe this is something God does for everyone.

Proverbs 29:18 says,

Where there is no vision, the people perish.

You need a vision for your life. Now there are going to be a lot of details that you can't know right away, and God doesn't even want you to know. If God were to show people everything that would happen once they started pursuing His vision for their lives, I guarantee you, many of them would run the other direction. They might say, "God, this is too big for me. There's too much suffering between here and there."

On the other hand, some people can get so impatient that they won't fulfill their obligation. They won't take the time to learn what they need to be able to grow and obtain the blessings God wants to put in their lives.

There are multiple reasons God doesn't show you everything, but He will give you a vision and point you in the direction that He wants you to go. God has to impart a vision to you before you can see His plan for your life come to pass.

I know that there are some people who are reading this right now who may be thinking, *Well, I don't have any vision for my life.* I'm saying this in love (Eph. 4:15), but that's one of the reasons your life isn't making a bigger impact. You just don't know God's vision for your life. But God does have a purpose and a vision for you!

Chapter 2

There Is a Plan for Your Life

For thou hast possessed my reins: thou hast covered me in my mother's womb. I will praise thee; for I am fearfully and wonderfully made: marvellous are thy works; and that my soul knoweth right well. My substance was not hid from thee, when I was made in secret, and curiously wrought in the lowest parts of the earth. Thine eyes did see my substance, yet being unperfect; and in thy book all my members were written, which in continuance were fashioned, when as yet there was none of them.

Psalm 139:13–16

Basically, this is saying all your days were written in the Lord's book before there was a single one of them. That means God had a plan for you when you were still in your mother's womb. It's not like He just winds you up and lets you go, and then you just do things your own way. God has a plan for each of us.

T. E. Lawrence (1888–1935)—the man commonly known as "Lawrence of Arabia"—said, "All men dream: but not equally. Those who dream by night in the dusty recesses of their minds wake in the day to find that it was vanity: but the dreamers of the day are dangerous men, for they may act their dreams with open eyes, to make it possible."[1]

That's not exactly the way we talk today, but it's a powerful truth. This is saying that all men dream but not equally. To some people, a dream doesn't mean anything because they wake up and it's gone. But then there are others who dream with their eyes open. In other words, this isn't talking about just something that takes place in your subconscious mind. This is talking about having a vision for your life.

People who have a vision live with a purpose. They aren't like pinballs who are launched and bounce around, living their lives by reacting to things. People who have a purpose for their lives—who are driven by visions and dreams—are dangerous men. Those are the men who change the course of the world.

If you don't get up in the morning with some degree of excitement about God's vision of where your life is going, then you're missing out on what life is really all about. You need to know God has a purpose for your life. You need to find out what that is and start moving in that direction.

God has a vision for every single one of us. He's never made a piece of junk or a failure. God never made anybody to just occupy space and then die. God has a plan for your life that is better than anything you could ever imagine. But in order for you to fulfill God's plan, you need to have some understanding about what He has in store for you. And I believe that's what the Lord did with Joseph.

These dreams showed Joseph he was going to be promoted above his brothers and that they would bow down to him—and that's exactly the way they took it! In Genesis 37:8, Joseph's brothers responded,

> *Shalt thou indeed reign over us? or shalt thou indeed have dominion over us? And they hated him yet the more for his dreams, and for his words.*

Don't Stir Up Strife

To understand why Joseph's brothers reacted the way they did, you have to know more about their family.

> *These are the generations of Jacob. Joseph, being seventeen years old, was feeding the flock with his brethren; and the lad was with the sons of Bilhah, and with the sons of Zilpah, his father's wives: and Joseph brought unto his father their evil report. Now Israel loved Joseph more than all his children, because he was the son of his old age: and he made him a coat of many colours. And when his brethren saw that their father loved him more than all his brethren, they hated him, and could not speak peaceably unto him.*
>
> Genesis 37:2–4

Jacob was Joseph's father. Earlier in his own life, Jacob wrestled with an angel (Gen. 32:24–32), and the angel changed his name to Israel (Gen. 32:28). So, throughout this story, Joseph's father is called Jacob *and* Israel.

Jacob had four wives. He took Rachel to be his wife after Laban deceived him into marrying her sister Leah first (Gen. 29–30). Rachel and Leah each had slaves, Bilhah and Zilpah. So, Jacob wound up with four wives and twelve sons. Joseph was the eleventh of the twelve sons (Gen. 30:24), the firstborn of Rachel, and had one younger brother named Benjamin who would play a significant role in his story (Gen. 35:18, 24).

If you go back to the story of Jacob, Rachel was his favorite wife. She was the one he really loved and wanted to marry (Gen. 29:18–21), but he wound up being tricked by his future father-in-law into marrying Leah, the older sister (Gen. 29:22–27). Jacob didn't like Leah and, because of this, God shut up the womb of Rachel so she couldn't have children right away (Gen. 29:31). Leah had four sons (Gen. 29:32–35), so Rachel gave her servant to Jacob so he could have children by her (Gen. 30:3–4).

Eventually, Rachel had two sons of her own, Joseph and Benjamin (Gen. 35:24). Because Joseph was the firstborn of his favorite wife, Jacob loved Joseph above all his other children (Gen. 37:3). Also, Joseph was the son of his old age.

A parent is not supposed to prefer one child over another regardless of whether one child is more beautiful, more talented, or more obedient than another. Again, many people fault Joseph for his brothers' envy, but instances like this show Jacob was the one at fault. As Genesis 37:4 says, *"And when his brethren saw that their father loved him more than all his brethren, they hated him, and could not speak peaceably unto him."* It was Israel's (Jacob's) preference for Joseph that turned the brothers against Joseph. They didn't even try to hide their envy and hatred for Joseph. One child should not be favored over his or her siblings like this.

James 3:16 says, *"For where envying and strife* is, *there is confusion and every evil work."* When you are envious of another person, that opens a door to anything the devil wants to do in your life. So, I don't believe the envy and jealousy these brothers had was caused by Joseph.

Confirming Dreams

Joseph was only seventeen years old when the events of Genesis 37:2–11 took place. There is no indication Joseph shared his dream with his brothers in a way to put them down. I believe it was just the innocence of a seventeen-year-old kid. God gave Joseph this dream, and it was about him being promoted to such a degree that even his brethren would come and bow down to him. I don't believe he was saying this in a way to rub their noses in it. He was just excited.

The worst anybody can attribute to Joseph in this situation is immaturity. It may be that if he had been more mature, he could have dissipated the special attention and love his father gave him, and he somehow could have mitigated his brothers' rejection of him. But his father's preference toward him is what put him in this situation with his brethren, and they hated him because of it.

You can see by the brothers' reaction that the interpretation of this dream was very clear to them. Joseph was going to prevail above his brothers, and they would someday bow down to him. This dream was repeated in a different way as a confirmation:

> *And he dreamed yet another dream, and told it his brethren, and said, Behold, I have dreamed a dream more; and, behold, the sun and the moon and the eleven stars made obeisance to me.*

> Genesis 37:9

Similarly, over in Genesis 41:32, Joseph stood before Pharaoh, interpreting his dreams. Joseph said,

> *And for that the dream was doubled unto Pharaoh twice; it is because the thing is established by God, and God will shortly bring it to pass.*

Joseph, as he was speaking under the inspiration of the Holy Spirit, said that when the same point is made by two different dreams it is established and will shortly come to pass. It cannot be changed.

Joseph had two dreams saying he was going to be exalted above his brothers. Because there were two dreams illustrating the same point, that meant the outcome couldn't be changed— it would happen. Then, Joseph shared the second dream with his father.

> [Jacob] *rebuked him, and said unto him, What* is *this dream that thou hast dreamed? Shall I and thy mother and thy brethren indeed come to bow down ourselves to thee to the earth?*
>
> Genesis 37:10b

It was very clear. Jacob was no stranger to dreams from God (Gen. 28:12 and 31:10–13), and he understood what Joseph's dream meant. It meant Joseph was going to be promoted over his father and mother (the sun and the moon), and his brothers (the eleven stars) were going to come and bow down to him.

Joseph was given direction by God that he was going to be promoted, and he held on to that. It's so important you don't let life's circumstances and problems derail you. This is one of the things about Joseph that just really inspires me: regardless of what happened to Joseph, he kept the dreams that God had put in his heart in front of him. It became motivation and a dominant force in his life. I don't believe he ever gave up on what God showed him.

It goes on to say, Joseph's *"brethren envied him; but his father observed the saying"* (Gen. 37:11). Even though Jacob rebuked Joseph for it, he observed what he said. Jacob held these things in his heart. This is the same thing that was said about Mary (Luke 2:48) when she rebuked Jesus (Luke 2:46) for being gone three days and speaking to the elders in the temple. Jesus rebuked his mother and said,

> *How is it that ye sought me? wist ye not that I must be about my Father's business?*
>
> Luke 2:49b

And it says that Mary *"kept all these sayings"* (Luke 2:51). She pondered them in her heart. Mary may not have understood everything about what was going on with Jesus, but she committed to think about it. I think this is the same thing that happened with Jacob when Joseph revealed his dream from God.

Seeing God's Vision

Every one of us has dreams. God reveals things to you, and He does it to prepare you. In between the moment God shows you the purpose for your life and when you see it come to pass, there is going to be a lot of time, and there is going to be opposition—there are going to be problems. And if you don't hold on to those dreams God has given you, I guarantee, it's going to make things much, much worse.

Your imagination is where you get a vision. It's your ability to see something on the inside that you can't see on the outside. You can't see with your physical eyes, but you can see it with your heart. It's with your heart you see God's vision for your life.

If you don't know where you're going, any old road will take you there. But when you have a vision, that determines which road you're going to take. It determines which direction you're going to go. If you don't have a vision for your life, you're just going with the flow, and you won't have a direction for your life. That's dangerous, and it's where Satan comes in and destroys people.

If you have a vision for what God wants your family to be, that will determine who you marry and the decisions you make. But if you have no vision for those things, you can just marry anybody. Then, after you get married, you may find out that decision didn't work out right—that your choice was wrong.

Praise God that Jamie and I committed our lives to the Lord before we ever got together. I knew the most important natural decision I would ever make was about who I married. I prayed about it long and hard, and God supernaturally put Jamie and me together. We were engaged to be married before we ever held hands. It's been a blessing.

Second Corinthians 6:14a says, *"Be ye not unequally yoked together."* We should avoid relationships where we are being more influenced by other people's negatives than they are by our positives. Marriage is one area where this principle is especially true. There is no closer union in life than the marriage relationship, but the Lord should be the most important person in a believer's life.

And remember, marriage should be based on a lot more than just the way a person looks. And yet, there are a lot of people who don't have that vision. They're just going after somebody who makes them feel good in the moment.

In the same way, there are many of you working jobs that you thought would make you a lot of money, or maybe there were good retirement benefits available. But there's more to life than just working a job, buying a house, having financial security, and things like that. That's a part of it, but there are people who just let material things drive them.

You need a vision. You need a purpose for your life that's bigger than a job, making money, finding a mate, or something like that. You need to know what God created you for. It's as if you are a round peg and you're trying to fit into a square hole. It's not going to work! You have to find the place that God made for you.

God's Purpose Revealed

I believe an important part of Joseph's story is the fact that God revealed a purpose for his life through these two dreams. The thing that kept Joseph on the right path was that he knew he had a destination. He was looking to go someplace, and the vision God planted in his heart propelled him to get there. As Psalm 105:19 says about Joseph, *"Until the time that his word came: the word of the LORD tried him."* The Amplified Bible's translation of that verse says, *"Until the time that his word [of prophecy regarding his brothers] came true, the word of the LORD tested and refined him."*

I can give personal testimony to verify this. When the Lord touched my life, he put a vision on the inside of me. I didn't have clarity, but I had a direction to go. And because of it, I started making decisions.

I actually wound up making some decisions that caused me to lose my student deferment from the military draft. I got drafted and sent to the war in Vietnam. Some people may think that was terrible, but it turned out to be one of the best things that ever happened to me because God had given me a direction.

I knew that I wasn't supposed to be a math major in college. I just knew that God had something more. I didn't know all the details, but I started moving in that direction. And it literally started moving me in such a way that I would've had to backslide from God to keep from being where I am today.

Proverbs 29:18 says, *"Where there is no vision, the people perish."* At least one modern translation says, *"Where there is no vision, the people cast off restraint"* (ASV). That means if you have a vision, you will restrain yourself. You discipline yourself because you've got some goal that you're headed toward.

Athletes who want to win a gold medal don't stay out and party all night. They train and eat a healthy diet. The goal of becoming a champion restrains what they do. But when a person doesn't have a vision, they cast off restraint. They just kind of go with the flow. Like water, they just seek the lowest level or choose the path of least resistance. They just do whatever is easiest.

Chapter 3

The Lord Will Protect You

And his brethren went to feed their father's flock in Shechem. And Israel said unto Joseph, Do not thy brethren feed the flock in Shechem? come, and I will send thee unto them. And he said to him, Here am I. And he said to him, Go, I pray thee, see whether it be well with thy brethren, and well with the flocks; and bring me word again. So he sent him out of the vale of Hebron, and he came to Shechem.

Genesis 37:12–14

Shechem is where Joseph's two older brothers, Simeon and Levi had gone in and killed every man in the town (Gen. 34:25–27)—hundreds of men—after their sister, Dinah, was raped by a man who lived there. They killed every single man and took all the women and children as slaves unto themselves (Gen. 34:29).

Simeon and Levi, the second- and the third-born sons of Jacob, were vile and mean men. Reuben, the firstborn, committed incest with his stepmother (Gen. 35:22), and because of that, he brought a curse upon himself (Gen. 49:3–4; Lev. 18:8, 29). The fourth-born son, Judah, wound up committing incest with his own daughter-in-law, and she got pregnant by him (Gen. 38:18–26). This just illustrates the kind of men Joseph's brothers were and may give you some more insight as to why they treated him the way they did.

> *And a certain man found him, and, behold, he was wandering in the field: and the man asked him, saying, What seekest thou? And he said, I seek my brethren: tell me, I pray thee, where they feed their flocks. And the man said, They are departed hence; for I heard them say, Let us go to Dothan. And Joseph went after his brethren, and found them in Dothan. And when they saw him afar off, even before he came near unto them, they conspired against him to slay him.*
>
> Genesis 37:15–18

Joseph couldn't find his brothers in Shechem, so he departed and found them in Dothan, *"And they said one to another, Behold, this dreamer cometh"* (Gen. 37:19). This is referring to Joseph's dreams where his brothers, father, and mother would bow down to him.

This kid was a thorn in these guys' side. These were ungodly men, and here was their little brother, already preferred by the father, saying he was going to be exalted over them. They were reacting in nothing but jealousy and pride. They hated him. Then, Joseph's brothers said,

> *Come now therefore, and let us slay him, and cast him into some pit, and we will say, Some evil beast hath devoured him: and we shall see what will become of his dreams.*
>
> Genesis 37:20

So, not only did these dreams have an impact on Joseph, but they were also a major influence on his brothers. They hated him because of these dreams, and it was a source of contention for them (Gen. 37:5, 8).

> *And Reuben heard* it, *and he delivered him out of their hands; and said, Let us not kill him. And Reuben said unto them, Shed no blood,* but *cast him into this pit that* is *in the wilderness, and lay no hand upon him; that he might rid him out of their hands, to deliver him to his father again.*
>
> Genesis 37:21–22

Now, Reuben had already shown he was not a godly man, but when he heard his brothers talk about killing Joseph, he at least had compassion on his little brother and his father. He was planning to deliver Joseph out of their hands and save his life. But even if Reuben had delivered Joseph right then, his brothers had it in their hearts to kill him. It would've just been a matter of time until something bad happened.

> *And it came to pass, when Joseph was come unto his brethren, that they stript Joseph out of his coat,* his *coat of* many *colours that* was *on him; and they took him, and cast him into a pit: and the pit* was *empty,* there *was no water in it. And they sat down to eat bread: and they lifted up their eyes and looked, and, behold, a company of Ishmeelites came from Gilead with their camels bearing spicery and balm and myrrh, going to carry* it *down to Egypt.*
>
> Genesis 37:23–25

Here they were, taking their little brother and casting him into a pit. They sought to kill him, but Reuben intervened. Maybe they weren't going to kill him, but just let him die of natural causes. And after all they had done to him, they just sat down and ate a meal. It was like they didn't even care. This reveals that Joseph's brothers were hardhearted people. I think sometimes people miss these things when they read Scripture.

God Works Through People

There were multiple reasons Joseph was sold into slavery, but I believe one of them was to get Joseph away from his brothers who were out to kill him. They would've killed him right then if Reuben hadn't stopped them. Sometimes when things happen, we just look at the negative side of everything. But there could be a silver lining to that cloud.

People think God just moves sovereignly and whatever happens is God's will. God does not move and control us like chess pieces. He doesn't just make things happen. He has to flow through people.

> *Now unto him that is able to do exceeding abundantly above all that we ask or think, according to the power that worketh in us.*
>
> Ephesians 3:20

God doesn't control everything. He doesn't cause trage-dies and wars. It's the evilness inside of men that causes these things.

> *From whence come wars and fightings among you? come they not hence, even of your lusts that war in your members? Ye lust, and have not: ye kill, and desire to have, and cannot obtain: ye fight and war, yet ye have not, because ye ask not. Ye ask, and receive not, because ye ask amiss, that ye may consume it upon your lusts.*
>
> James 4:1–3

God did not cause Joseph's brethren to hate him and to think about killing him. But even though all of these negative things were going on, God can still use people and get His will

29

accomplished. It's not that God controls people against their will, but he can take people and use them in spite of themselves.

> *And Judah said unto his brethren, What profit is it if we slay our brother, and conceal his blood? Come, and let us sell him to the Ishmeelites, and let not our hand be upon him; for he is our brother and our flesh. And his brethren were content.*
>
> Genesis 37:26–27

Joseph's brothers weren't feeding their flocks in the place where they told their father they would be. Joseph had brought an "evil report" to their father before (Gen. 37:2), and they weren't about to let him do it again. When they saw him coming, they conspired to kill him. Reuben at least intervened to save his life, but they still threw him into a pit without food or water.

Judah knew this was not the way to treat their brother. These verses reveal he knew better in his heart. Every person in their heart—no matter what they're living like—knows right from wrong (Rom. 1:18–20). Now, you can deaden yourself to that. You can sear your conscience (1 Tim. 4:2), but you don't start out that way. Everybody knows right from wrong.

> *Then there passed by Midianites merchantmen; and they drew and lifted up Joseph out of the pit, and sold Joseph*

to the Ishmeelites for twenty pieces *of silver: and they brought Joseph into Egypt.*

Genesis 37:28

The Ishmeelites and Midianites were on their way down to Egypt, and God laid it on the brothers' hearts to sell Joseph to them. Judah knew that killing his younger brother was wrong, and so he considered that it might be better to sell Joseph and make some money. That way, he and his brothers wouldn't have his blood on their hands.

First Timothy 6:10 says, *"the love of money is the root of all evil."* God didn't put this love of money in people, but He can use it. See, people don't actually love money—they don't lust after colored paper or minted coins. They love what money can do for them. They either love the things that money can buy, or they love the power, influence, and security that money provides.

In this case, instead of just killing Joseph to satisfy their own jealousy, the brothers saw an opportunity to profit from his misery. Rather than let the brothers kill Joseph, God took their own carnal nature—their love for money—and used it to get Joseph out of the pit and sell him into slavery. It ended up saving his life.

As I mentioned earlier, I believe one of the reasons God moved on Joseph's brothers to sell him into slavery was to get him away from them. These were very ungodly men, and I believe God did it as much to save Joseph's life as he did for any other purpose. So, it was actually to his benefit. God didn't just sovereignly make it happen, though. God took the brothers' own greed for money and used it to preserve Joseph's life by moving on them to sell him into slavery.

Guilty by Association

And Reuben returned unto the pit; and, behold, Joseph was not in the pit; and he rent his clothes. And he returned unto his brethren, and said, The child is not; and I, whither shall I go? And they took Joseph's coat, and killed a kid of the goats, and dipped the coat in the blood; and they sent the coat of many colours, and they brought it to their father; and said, This have we found: know now whether it be thy son's coat or no.

Genesis 37:29–32

This was total deception. Even though the brothers didn't kill Joseph, they lied about what they did to him and misrepresented it to their father. They put blood on Joseph's coat and implied that he had been killed by some wild beast. Of course, they knew it wasn't true. And even though Reuben wanted to deliver Joseph back to Jacob, he went along with this ruse. Reuben knew that Joseph had been sold into slavery, and he kept quiet.

Most people know that you can be guilty by association. For example, if somebody robs a bank and you just drive the getaway car, you will have some responsibility. You may not have been the one who went into the bank and stole the money, but you'll be put into prison too. If somebody was killed in the robbery, then you are also an accessory to murder. So, Reuben, even though he wasn't the one who sold Joseph to the Ishmeelites and Midianites, was guilty of participating in his brothers' plot and went along with their lie.

Let's look at how Jacob responded to the story.

And [Jacob] *knew it, and said,* It is *my son's coat; an evil beast hath devoured him; Joseph is without doubt rent in pieces. And Jacob rent his clothes, and put sackcloth upon his loins, and mourned for his son many days. And all his sons and all his daughters rose up to comfort him; but he refused to be comforted; and he said, For I will go down into the grave unto my son mourning. Thus his father wept for him.*

Genesis 37:33–35

Jacob made a major mistake right here by just assuming something based on what it looked like. Here was a coat that had blood on it, and he assumed it was Joseph's blood. He just swallowed his sons' lies—hook, line, and sinker. You cannot let circumstances and what things look like direct your life. You need to have a vision and purpose from God.

If Jacob had just gone back and remembered the dream Joseph shared with him, he would have realized that it had not been fulfilled. He would have at least had a second thought about what his sons were trying to tell him.

Hold on to Dreams

I remember on March 4, 2001, when Jamie and I were told our son Jonathan Peter died. I could have gotten into sorrow and let circumstances direct my response, but I remembered prophecies given about our son that had not yet come to pass in his life. So, for these prophecies to be fulfilled, Peter had to live. We just began praising the Lord and thanking Him for all the good things He'd already done and what He was doing. And when we arrived at the hospital, our oldest son Joshua met us at the door and said, "I don't know what happened, but right after I got off the phone with you, they said Peter sat up and started talking." Praise the Lord!

I know it wasn't the same exact situation, but Jacob should have held on to Joseph's dreams. He could have said, "Well, God gave Joseph a dream, and it hasn't come to pass yet. I know it looks like he was eaten by a wild beast, but I am going to trust God." Instead, he disregarded God's vision for his son's life and said, *"Joseph is without doubt rent in pieces"* (Gen. 37:33), then went to mourning for him.

At any point, one of those brothers could have seen their father suffering and stepped in to say, "Joseph isn't really dead; he's alive." But they didn't. And, as we'll see later, they kept that lie going for twenty-two years, letting their father grieve all that time. Again, that just goes to show how hardhearted Joseph's brothers really were.

I can go back to my life and say that there are many times when it looked like I just made a mistake choosing to be a minister. For a long time, it just didn't work. It looked like Jamie and I had just messed up. We were living in poverty. We were struggling, and bad things were happening.

Jamie's dad even came to me once and said, "Look, you're a nice guy, but you just aren't making it as a preacher. You need to go do something else." And I guarantee you, if I would've just interpreted things based on circumstances, I would have never stayed with the ministry. But today, praise God, we're having an influence around the world! We're touching people and taking the Gospel farther and deeper than ever before. That's all because I had a word from the Lord, and I followed that instead of making decisions based on our circumstances.

You need to get a word from God. Jacob, at the very least, should have prayed about this and sought God. But no, he just jumped to a conclusion. And because of that, he grieved and refused to be comforted.

Jacob grieved for twenty-two years, thinking his son was dead. He would have grieved even longer if Joseph hadn't revealed himself to his brothers. Jacob said, *"I will go down into the grave unto my son mourning"* (Gen. 37:35). But he was mourning over something that wasn't true. Joseph wasn't dead. Jacob's son ended up prospering in Egypt, and he eventually got to share in that; but he went through a lot of grief that he didn't have to go through.

Overcome Adversity

There are a lot of people who suffer and don't allow themselves to be comforted after something bad happens. I'm not saying something tragic didn't happen—they may have lost a loved one, a marriage, a business, or something else—but a person doesn't have to be of the mindset where they refuse to be comforted. That's just wrong.

My brother was married for about thirty years, and then his wife died in a car wreck. After that, he just went into a tailspin. I called and talked to him, and he was just suffering—struggling to survive. But one day, I called him, and he was just different. He was back to his old self. He was normal.

I remember asking, "What happened? It's like somebody just turned on a switch in you." And he said the Lord spoke to him and told him, "You either need to dig a hole next to your dead wife, crawl in, and die, or you need to get on with your life." That really blessed me, and I've shared that story many times.

There are terrible things that happen in life. I understand we live in a fallen world, but what are you going to do? Are you going to go down to your grave, mourning over something that's already passed? I don't believe that's the right approach. You just have to get over it, trust God, rejoice in Him, and get on with living.

I've gone back and studied a lot of history. One of the major differences between the 2020 coronavirus pandemic and the 1918 Spanish flu was how people responded. If you just go back and look at people's attitudes, they were emotionally stronger in the past. It seemed like people panicked during the 2020 pandemic and operated totally in fear.

More than three years after the first diagnosis of COVID-19, when the public health emergency ended in the United States, there were 765 million cases reported worldwide, resulting in about seven million deaths (or a death rate of less than 1 percent).[2] The world's population at the time was about eight billion people,[3] so less than 10 percent of the population was infected by COVID.

By contrast, the Spanish flu was much more lethal. Historians show that of the 500 million people who were infected by Spanish flu, at least fifty million died (or a death rate of at least 10 percent).[4] The estimated world population in 1920, three years after the outbreak, was just under two billion people,[5] which means around 25 percent of people were infected. And yet, back in those days, they didn't shut everything down. They didn't respond in fear and just got on with life. People had a different attitude.

Revelation 12:11 says, *"And they overcame him by the blood of the Lamb, and by the word of their testimony,"* and most people just stop right there and put a period. They just say, "I'm going to overcome the devil by the blood of the Lamb, and the word of my testimony," and that's good; but the verse goes on to say, *"and they loved not their lives unto the death."*

I guarantee you, if you're ever going to overcome the devil by the blood of the Lamb and the word of your testimony, you've got to get to a place that you love not your life to the death. You have to love God and commit yourself to what He has called you to do more than you love yourself.

But these days, just like it says in 2 Timothy 3:2–4, people are *"lovers of their own selves . . .* [and] *lovers of pleasures more than lovers of God."* Because of this, there are a lot of weak people because their lives are all about them. And if what God has called them to do is going to cost them something, they just fall apart like a two-dollar suitcase when persecution and tribulation comes.

So, here was Jacob, just refusing to be comforted, nursing his hurts. He was going to grieve the rest of his life, thinking it was honoring Joseph. But it didn't help Joseph a bit. Instead, it hurt Jacob. He lost twenty-two years of his life by operating in grief. The Bible says Joseph's brothers tried to comfort him, but Jacob refused to be comforted.

Now, think about Joseph's brothers. Reuben wanted to deliver Joseph out of that pit and bring him back to his father. He didn't want to sell Joseph into slavery the way his brothers did. But he still saw his father grieving and didn't try to stop it by just telling the truth. And what's more, Reuben and his brothers were still living with their father. It's not like they moved away and didn't see each other. They all lived together. Every single day for twenty-two years, they saw their father grieving but wouldn't tell the truth—that Joseph was still alive. That's just terrible!

Chapter 4

God Determines Your Value

And the Midianites sold [Joseph] *into Egypt unto Potiphar, an officer of Pharaoh's, and captain of the guard.*

Genesis 37:36

Think about the Ishmeelites and Midianites. They bought Joseph for twenty pieces of silver and sold him. We don't know what they sold him for, but it was a bad deal on their part. They didn't understand who Joseph really was. This guy was going to be the leader of Egypt someday.

Sometimes we undervalue people by looking at who they are in the moment. We don't see them for what their real potential is. In 2 Corinthians 5:16, the apostle Paul wrote, *"know we no man after the flesh."* We have to know people by the spirit. We need to let the Lord help us look past the way someone looks, the way they're dressed, or the circumstances that they're in at that moment. We need to see people for who God sees them to be.

And Joseph was brought down to Egypt; and Potiphar, an officer of Pharaoh, captain of the guard, an Egyptian,

41

> *bought him of the hands of the Ishmeelites, which had*
> *brought him down thither. And the* Lord *was with*
> *Joseph, and he was a prosperous man; and he was in the*
> *house of his master the Egyptian.*
>
> Genesis 39:1–2

According to the Bible, Joseph was a prosperous man, but here he was being sold into slavery. Again, this just reflects how people look at things totally different than the way God does. These Ishmeelites and Midianites thought that they made some money off Joseph, but they missed one of the biggest sales that they could have ever had. If they really knew who Joseph was, they could've gotten a lot more.

The way that they sold slaves was to strip them totally naked. They would just stand there without one stitch of clothing on so the person who's buying them could actually see what they were getting for their money. So, here's Joseph, standing totally naked with his clothes next to him, and there's Potiphar, who was probably dressed to the nines; he probably wore all kinds of fancy clothes, jewels, and gold. But the Bible didn't say Potiphar was a prosperous man. Joseph was the one who was prosperous, even though he was standing there totally naked, because God sees things differently than the way we see things.

You may see yourself in a situation where you're behind financially. You may be in a situation where your body has sickness. And other people may see you, pity you, and have a negative opinion of you. But really, none of those things matter. What matters is how God sees you and what His purpose is for your life.

How You See Yourself

When the Israelites were supposed to go into the Promised Land, they sent out spies (Num. 13:17–20). At first, they came back with a good report.

> *And they went and came to Moses, and to Aaron, and to all the congregation of the children of Israel, unto the wilderness of Paran, to Kadesh; and shewed them the fruit of the land. And they told him, and said, We came unto the land whither thou sentest us, and surely it floweth with milk and honey; and this is the fruit of it.*
>
> Numbers 13:26–27

They had one cluster of grapes that was so big it had to be carried on a pole between two men (Num. 13:23). We can't even imagine that today. But then they said,

> *And there we saw the giants, the sons of Anak, which come of the giants: and we were in our own sight as grasshoppers, and so we were in their sight.*
>
> Numbers 13:33

If they would've just stopped with saying that the giants saw them as grasshoppers, they might have been okay. But they went on to say, *"and so we were in their sight"* (Num. 13:33). It doesn't matter how others see us. What's important is how we see ourselves. The moment they agreed with the giants, they were doomed.

As a matter of fact, after the Israelites had camped in the wilderness for a generation and finally moved in to take the walled city of Jericho, Rahab told them,

> *I know that the LORD hath given you the land, and that your terror is fallen upon us, and that all the inhabitants of the land faint because of you. For we have heard how the LORD dried up the water of the Red sea for you, when ye came out of Egypt. . . . And as soon as we had heard* these things, *our hearts did melt, neither did there remain any more courage in any man, because of you: for the LORD your God, he is God in heaven above, and in earth beneath.*
>
> Joshua 2:9–11

It really shouldn't matter how you think other people see you. What's more important is who your God is and how you see yourself in light of what Jesus has already done. Actually, a negative view of yourself is rooted in pride and self-centeredness.

I remember a man who spoke with me after a service in Pueblo, Colorado, years ago. He said, "I don't have any pride. I have just the opposite—low self-esteem." I responded by telling him that low self-esteem is really just another form of pride. It's the result of focusing on yourself compared to others and then concluding that you just don't measure up. It's still just all about you. I'll tell you, people who are all wrapped up in themselves make a pretty small package.

God Is with You

Joseph was being sold as a slave, and most people today would have looked at his situation and said, "That's terrible! He's just reduced to nothing." There Joseph was, the favorite son of a very wealthy man back in the land of Israel, who became a slave. He had just gone from the heights to the depths. And yet God said he was a prosperous man. I think Joseph also believed that he was a prosperous man because he held on to those dreams. He knew that somehow or another he was going to come through this thing, regardless of what the situation looked like.

Genesis 39:2a says, *"And the LORD was with Joseph,"* and Joseph knew it. If the Lord is with you, then who can be against you (Rom. 8:31)? It doesn't matter what your circumstances are. It doesn't matter what the doctor or banker says. It doesn't matter what anyone says! If you could hold on to the fact that God is with you—if you could get a vision of what God wants to do in your life—it is just a matter of time until you see His will come to pass. But this is where you've got to fight the battle.

Before you see the end results, you've got to remain in faith. You've got to walk in faith even when you can't see it in the natural (2 Cor. 5:7). By faith, you've got to be able to see the things God has shown to you. Because the Lord was with Joseph, he was a prosperous man.

> *And his master saw that the LORD was with him, and that the LORD made all that he did to prosper in his hand.*
>
> Genesis 39:3

In the same way the Lord was with Joseph, He is also with you and me. Scripture says He'll never leave us nor forsake us (Heb. 13:5). But it's not always evident to people that the Lord is with them. The reason for that is because they aren't always walking in faith. They're walking in fear or bitterness.

Joseph could've been bitter. He could've thought, *I went from being the favorite son to being hated by my brothers, thrown into the pit, and sold into slavery.* He could've sulked and been depressed. I can guarantee, those are natural things that most people let dominate them. But Joseph kept believing God was with him. And because of that, God's presence and favor on Joseph's life was manifest to his master.

Don't Look at Circumstances

You've got to walk in faith and believe God is with you even when circumstances make it look like that's not true. If you believe and faint not, in due season, you will reap (Gal. 6:9). But if you faint along the way—if you get discouraged because things aren't working out the way you hoped they would—you'll never see God's will come to pass. That doesn't mean God didn't have a purpose for you, but there is a part for you to play. You've got to stand in faith.

Joseph was standing in faith. And everything he did, God made it prosper in his hands. In the same way, I believe that regardless of what I do, whatever I set my hand unto is going to prosper (Deut. 28:12). I don't believe that because I'm so great. I believe it because of the favor of God on me.

Many years ago, I got into a situation where I owed my landlord some money. I told him I didn't have the money, and he said I could work off the debt. He owned a photography studio and was about to lose his business because he was over-extended. He had some people quit their jobs, and he couldn't do all the work, So, I got in there, and I just started praying and believing God. Because of that, I was able to prosper, and this man saw the blessing of God on my life. As a matter of fact, he offered me 50 percent of his business only two months after I started.

When I left there and prepared to move to Pritchett, Colorado, the owner of that photography studio asked me if I would train my replacement. So, this guy came in, I told him all the things I knew, and he just blurted out, "How do you do this?" He panicked because he didn't really know how I did everything so well. Finally, I just had to tell him.

I said, "I pray in tongues and God tells me how to adjust and what each picture needs to be developed, and that's how I do it." And again, this guy just panicked. He said "Well, I don't pray in tongues!" I said, "I can tell you how to pray in tongues. I can pray with you so you can receive the baptism of the Holy Spirit." I couldn't explain it any better because it was through prayer and believing God's Word that I was successful. I had no ability to develop photographs on my own. God's favor was on me.

I'm not just saying these things because I'm special. I'm saying that I have been in situations where I had to go do something that I had no ability to do, but I prayed over it. Because God was with me, I prospered. Everything I put my hand to is blessed.

This is what happened to Joseph. He had a vision. He knew that he wasn't going to be a slave forever. And because of that, he was still believing God.

Have an Excellent Spirit

And Joseph found grace in his sight, and he served him: and he made him overseer over his house, and all that *he had he put into his hand. And it came to pass from the time* that *he had made him overseer in his house, and over all that he had, that the* LORD *blessed the Egyptian's house for Joseph's sake; and the blessing of the* LORD *was upon all that he had in the house, and in the field. And he left all that he had in Joseph's hand; and he knew not ought he had, save the bread which he did eat. And Joseph was a goodly* person, *and well favoured.*

Genesis 39:4–6

Notice he served the man who bought him. There are many people who, if they were taken and made a slave, would just sit down and suck their thumb and talk about how bad their situation was. They'd be depressed, discouraged, and just give up and say, "What's the use?"

Joseph could have complained. He could have been discouraged. He could have quit, and he would've never seen any of his dreams come to pass. But even though Joseph was a slave, he was going to be the best slave that Potiphar ever had. Here was Joseph, serving his master with such excellence, that Potiphar made him *"overseer over his house, and all* that *he had he put into his hand"* (Gen. 37:4).

49

Again, this didn't just happen automatically. God didn't sovereignly promote Joseph in Potiphar's house. This happened because Joseph was still holding on to God's vision for his life, and he was serving this man with excellence. He was not sitting down, griping and complaining. Joseph was giving it all that he had—as a slave! And because of that, God not only blessed Joseph, but he also blessed his master's house.

Potiphar didn't even pay any attention to his financial or business dealings because he trusted Joseph so much. I guarantee, someone in a position of authority like Potiphar is not going to trust a person who's bitter. They're not going to give responsibility to a person who's just given up—someone who's just going along to get along. Joseph was a person who had excellence, and here he was as a slave still serving God. He still believed his current situation was not going to be the end of his life. He was holding on to those visions God gave him.

We should quit praying, "God, change my circumstances," but instead pray, "God, change me so I can rise up to the occasion when opportunity comes and have the character to be able to handle it." That's really important.

Have you given up? Are you depressed, thinking about all of the things that have gone wrong in your life, or do you have a vision? Are you pressing on toward that vision regardless of what happens? In my life, God has spoken to me through Joseph so many times. There were times I felt like quitting.

There were things that I was seeing in the natural that didn't match the vision I had on the inside of me. And yet, I didn't know how to do it any differently. I just kept doing what I knew to do and kept serving the Lord the best I knew how.

There are some of you who have given up and are discouraged. But you just need to build yourself up. You need to encourage yourself (1 Sam. 30:6). You need to stir yourself up or you're going to sink to the bottom. You need to have a vision. You need to get yourself up and say, "I don't care what this day is like, I'm going to give it all I have! I'm going to bless somebody! I'm going to go in and make my employer prosper!" Even if you feel like you are not receiving enough in return from others, that doesn't matter. You go ahead and do what's right because God will bless you!

Be a Blessing

I had a man come to me one time who was complaining about his job. He had been working for a man for many years and he was the first—and, for a time, only—employee this guy had. As the business prospered, the owner hired other people, promoted them, and put them in positions above his first employee. So, this guy who came to me was still the lowest-paid person in the entire company but had been there longer than anybody else.

He was just griping and complaining as he was telling me about his situation. I could tell he was bitter. He was ready to give up and quit. But I told this man his own attitude was the real problem. I said, "You aren't serving that guy with excellence. You're bitter. You are just working there to get the money, but you aren't doing it with the right attitude."

I told this man he needed to pray and change this attitude. I said, "You need to forgive your boss. You need to serve him. You need to make him prosperous." So, when he went back to work, he changed his attitude and started working hard at his job.

A few weeks later, that same man came to me and said, "You're never going to believe what happened." His boss came through his workplace one day and said something that would have normally angered him. But instead of reacting in bitterness, this man just said, "I forgive you," and went back to his work.

His boss walked away, but then came back to ask, "What do you forgive me for? What do I have to be forgiven of?" And his employee just told him, but he didn't do it out of bitterness. The man said, "I'm your oldest employee, and yet I'm the least paid. You've promoted all these other people, and I had a bad attitude about it. But I've repented, and I'm going to serve you. I'm going to give you everything I've got."

As it turned out, this man's boss was having marital problems. He had this man pray with him and helped him. The man who had come to me bitter and complaining about his boss ended up being promoted over all the other employees—and his salary was nearly doubled! It was all because he changed his attitude.

You may be in a bad situation, but you don't have to become bitter and complain. That is not what Joseph did. Joseph was serving his master with his whole heart. And because of it, the blessing of God was evident and manifest in his life. His master promoted him to the degree that Potiphar didn't even know anything that was going on in his house. That's how much he trusted Joseph. He was promoted because he wasn't griping. He wasn't bitter. He was serving. I believe Joseph had a good attitude.

If you've allowed yourself to become bitter, lost your vision, given up, and you're just drifting with the tide, that's not the way to live. Any dead fish can float downstream. But you need to turn around and start swimming upstream. You need to have a goal and a vision for your life, and you need to start moving toward what God called you to do.

I take tremendous encouragement from Joseph. Here's a man who was in a situation worse than I've ever been in. I've never been sold into slavery. I've never had my brother try and kill me. I've never had any of the things that happened to Joseph happen to me. And if Joseph could be faithful—if he could be positive and still operate in excellence in a situation that is worse than anything you or I might face—then certainly born-again, Spirit-baptized believers should be able to endure the problems we face with a positive attitude. This should encourage you!

Chapter 5

Maintain Your Integrity

At the end of Genesis 39:6, it says, *"Joseph was a goodly person and well favored."* In other modern translations it says, *"Joseph was well-built and handsome."* As a general rule, it is not the handsome and well-built, or people that have great talents and abilities, who are used by God. The reason is so that no flesh would glory in His presence (1 Cor. 1:29).

In 1 Corinthians 1:26–28, the apostle Paul wrote,

> *For ye see your calling, brethren, how that not many wise men after the flesh, not many mighty, not many noble,* are called: *but God hath chosen the foolish things of the world to confound the wise; and God hath chosen the weak things of the world to confound the things which are mighty; and base things of the world, and things which are despised, hath God chosen,* yea, *and things which are not, to bring to nought things that are.*

God often chooses people who don't have everything in the natural going for them, so that when He flows through them, He gets the credit instead of that person. But it's also important to recognize that God is not against people who are well built, handsome, and have everything going for them.

Joseph is an example of a person who, in the natural, had positive things going for him, and yet God used him. God is not against people who have great talents and abilities. It's just that people who have those talents and abilities tend to depend upon themselves instead of depending upon God. He often has to find somebody like me who has no great natural talents or abilities.

One time, a man contacted us who was called into ministry but wasn't pursuing what God had for him. After he saw me minister, he wrote to us and said, "I figured if you could do it, anybody could!" Later, he mentioned some other notable ministers who were from my part of the country and said, "Why is it that God always seems to use hicks from Texas?" And my response was, "Because hicks from Texas know their limitations and are God-dependent!" Amen!

As you can tell, I'm not the most qualified person to do what I do. Some may only see me as a hick from Texas and a college dropout. But the Lord has used me to raise up Charis Bible College campuses all around the world that are training ministers and equipping believers. In the natural, it doesn't make sense. But God saw my heart, not my education (or lack thereof).

We've all sinned and fallen short of the glory of God (Rom. 3:23). I'm here to tell you God hasn't had a qualified person working for Him yet. Humble yourself and do as Joseph did. The Lord isn't looking for a silver vessel, just a surrendered one.

Situational Ethics

And it came to pass after these things, that his master's wife cast her eyes upon Joseph; and she said, Lie with me.

Genesis 39:7

"Lie with me," is an old English way to say, "Have sex with me." Here Joseph was, serving his master with excellence, with everything in the household entrusted to him, and Potiphar's wife was trying to seduce him.

Most people would be bitter if they had been the favored son, owned a coat of many colors, and were so prosperous that they had everything, but then were sold into slavery. They'd be angry. Now, imagine if somebody like that was presented with the opportunity to compromise. At this time, Joseph was a virgin—he never had a relationship with a woman—and here he is in a foreign land, basically forgotten by his family. Now this woman was making herself available to him. For a lot of men, this would've been a difficult situation.

The only reason that most people have any standard of morality is because of the potential consequences that come with it. I remember reading where someone left a billfold on the sidewalk that had cash in it, along with a name and contact number. They did this as a test and had hidden cameras set up to watch what people would do. People would stop, pick up the billfold, and see the money in it.

Out of all of the people who picked up the billfold, there was just a small percentage who tried to return it using the information inside. But most people would look both ways to see if anybody else was watching before they pocketed the cash and walked off. As these people started walking away with the money, somebody would stop them, tell them it was part of a test, and ask, "If you had a contact number, why didn't you want to contact somebody? Why didn't you turn it in?" Many of the people who took the money said the reason they didn't return the billfold is because they didn't think anybody would see them—there wouldn't be any consequences. In other words, that's called situational ethics.

When I was serving in Vietnam, there was another guy there who grew up with me. We weren't close, but we knew each other. We went to church together and knew each other our entire lives. And there we were, both in Vietnam together. We weren't in the exact same spot, but we saw each other often.

Every so often, the U.S. military would bring the troops out of the field for what they called a "stand down." And for three days, they would give them all the alcohol they could drink. They also brought in women and put on a musical show that was sexually oriented. It turned out, those women just happened to be prostitutes, so a person could have all of the booze, drugs, and sex they wanted for three days. And it was the U.S. government who did this for the troops.

This man I grew up with wasn't a fanatic about God, but he was born again. He would've never participated in anything like that back in the states because it would've been a reflection on his family. But in Vietnam, he did. Back home, it could've affected him in many different ways. But on the other side of the world, there was a risk of getting killed at any time. A person serving over there didn't know if they would get out of Vietnam alive, and certainly nobody back home was ever going to know about the immoral behavior. So, there were a lot of guys who wouldn't have ever lived that way in the states, but in Vietnam they just let themselves go. They indulged every single appetite that they had.

I was in a company of 200 people, and every time they'd bring us back for stand down, I was the only person who did not go to the shows and participate. I was a chaplain's assistant, and my chaplain got drunk, got up on the stage, and tried to strip naked and have sex with these women in front of 200 people. And here I was, the only person who didn't participate.

It's just like what Joseph faced. His master's wife was saying, "Come, lie with me." And he could have gotten by with it.

He could have thought, *Well, I deserve at least some gratification, and who is going to know?* Certainly, the master's wife wasn't going to tell on him because it would've meant her head too. He could've gotten by with it.

Most people who operate according to situational ethics would think the same way. They'd only do what's right if they knew they were going to be held accountable. Sad to say, that's the way most people are. They don't have enough integrity to do what's right, whether somebody's watching or not.

This is just my own personal opinion, but I think a lot of post-traumatic stress disorder isn't just from the torments of war. The typical soldier indulges in sinful behavior with prostitutes, dope, and alcohol. They do things in war that they would never do back home—where they would be accountable to a spouse or a family, father or mother, sister or brother, or someone else. Their guilt and shame are just eating them up on the inside. So, when they come home, they may struggle with what they saw during battle, but I think that there's also a lot of guilt over all the other things that were done.

Relationship with God

But he refused, and said unto his master's wife, Behold, my master wotteth not what is with me in the house, and he hath committed all that he hath to my hand; there is none greater in this house than I; neither hath he kept back any thing from me but thee, because thou art *his wife: how then can I do this great wickedness, and sin against God?*

Genesis 39:8–9

What Joseph said to his master's wife speaks loud and clear. It wasn't about him. It was about serving. He actually honored his master. Potiphar, according to everything we know, didn't believe in the God of Joseph. He could have been a very ungodly man, but Joseph had a responsibility, and he honored his master. Then he went on to say, "*how then can I do this great wickedness, and sin against God?*"

God spoke this to me big time when I was in Vietnam. Like I said, there were all kinds of temptations available, and there is a desire in people to be accepted. There is a desire to not stand out and have people criticize you. I had people in Vietnam who would always call me "Preacher" and make fun of me. I had people treat me like the plague. They would see me coming and turn around to walk in the other direction. I'll tell you, if you like rejection, something's wrong with you. I didn't enjoy any of that. And there was a desire to be accepted around these other people. There was a desire to be a part of something.

I remember being on stand down back in Chu Lai on the South China Sea, which was my division headquarters. I could hear all of the music and yelling going on in that pavilion, but

I would just sit on the beach while all that debauchery went on around me. All of that noise was like a magnet drawing me because I wanted to be accepted. And yet, God spoke to me through Joseph's words, "*how could I do this great wickedness and sin against God?*" But this friend of mine, who had the same upbringing as I did, he wound up giving in because satisfying his flesh was more important to him than his relationship with God.

If the only reason you're doing what's right is because you're going to be answerable to somebody, then I can guarantee Satan will put you in a position to compromise. This happens all the time. If you have a relationship with God, it's not about whether or not you get caught; it's about what God says.

This is what kept me when I was in Vietnam. I felt the temptation and the draw to be a part of what other people were doing—to be accepted by them. But I loved God more than I loved people. And I remember God using this verse to speak to me. I thought, *God, I can't do this. I don't care whether anybody else ever knows or not because You know. I'm not going to live this way. I'm not going to take their free booze. I'm not going to take the free drugs and sex. I'm not doing this stuff.* And it was because I had a relationship with God.

I was scheduled to speak at a Christian school one time, and while I was waiting, I read their promotional literature. The number-one thing they promoted was positive peer pressure; that's how they were advertising their school. It was a Christian school and, because there were Christian kids there, they were going to use peer pressure to influence the students in a positive way, unlike public school where there was negative peer pressure. Even though I understood the point that they were making, that's still not the right way to do things because you're training them to be a part of a group.

Now, if it's a Christian group, that's great! But you're training people to have a herd mentality and do what it takes to be accepted by everybody. What happens when you take them out of that Christian environment and put them in a situation like I faced in Vietnam? What if they are involved in something where there are no restrictions, and they could participate in all the ungodliness they wanted. Well, the same peer pressure used in that Christian school would cause those people to go along with others just to get along. That's wrong! Peer pressure should not be the motivation for anything. It's all about having a personal relationship with God.

Do What Is Right

This is one of the things about Joseph that just really ministered to me. Joseph was going to honor the Lord who had given him two dreams about what He was going to do in his life. That's integrity. Proverbs 11:3a says, *The integrity of the upright shall guide them.* What that means is, if you have made a commitment to God, you are going to serve and do what's right whether it's popular or not. That sets up boundaries, and it makes you live within them. It won't matter whether other people change their standards. You're going to do what's right.

Joseph had integrity, and that was going to limit what he could do. He was honoring his master, but the biggest thing was, *"how* [could] *I do this great wickedness, and sin against God?"* This ought to be something that gets down on the inside of you as you read this. When you make a decision, your first thought should be, *God, it doesn't matter what anybody else says. I am going to do what's right, and I am not going to sin against You.*

People may say, "Don't go out and participate in sexual immorality because there are sexually transmitted diseases! It's like playing Russian roulette. It's just a matter of time until you come down with some kind of a disease." That may be true, but that should not be the real deterrent.

It's true that there are physical consequences to sin, but the real motivation to be obedient ought to be your relationship with God. Even if there were a cure for HIV/AIDS, it would still be wrong to engage in homosexuality because it doesn't honor God.

Jesus said, *"But from the beginning of the creation God made them male and female"* (Mark 10:6). Marriage is between a man and a woman, and it doesn't matter what the culture says. There are many Christians who are caving on this issue because society has embraced homosexuality. They basically put a stamp of approval on it. And even those who don't agree with that lifestyle believe Christians are wrong to say that homosexuality is wrong.

It is not popular to stand on what the Word of God says. And a lot of Christians are caving because of this herd mentality and a desire to be accepted. That's just wrong. You've got to recognize, it's your personal accountability to God that gives you character, integrity, and boundaries for your life.

Joseph had a relationship with God. He had shown Joseph that he was going to be promoted and that his brothers would come and bow down before him. Joseph had a vision that restrained him and that kept him on the right path. He refused to deviate from it.

Flee from Temptation

And it came to pass, as she spake to Joseph day by day, that he hearkened not unto her, to lie by her, or to be with her. And it came to pass about this time, that Joseph went into the house to do his business; and there was none of the men of the house there within. And she caught him by his garment, saying, Lie with me: and he left his garment in her hand, and fled, and got him out.

Genesis 39:10–12

The Scripture says, *"Resist the devil, and he will flee from you"* (James 4:7), but it also says, *"Flee fornication"* (1 Cor. 6:18). You can't just flee from the devil; you have to resist him first. But you can flee from temptation. Most people are resisting temptation but fleeing from the devil, which is the exact opposite of what God says.

You should flee from situations that bring you into temptation. You should flee from movies and other things that plant sinful desires in your heart. You shouldn't expose yourself to things that promote adultery, fornication, and other ungodly things for entertainment. You need to be focused on God. You need to flee sexual sin and *then* resist the devil. Joseph fled from his master's wife. He refused to even be around her.

But even though *"he hearkened not unto her, to lie by her, or to be with her,"* something demanded he go into the house and conduct the business his master had given him. And while he was there, it says, *"he came into the house to do his business; and* there was *none of the men of the house there within."*

Apparently in previous times, there were other people in the house who prevented him from being alone with Potiphar's wife, but this time nobody else was around. So, *"she caught him by his garment, saying, Lie with me: and he left his garment in her hand, and fled, and got him out."* Joseph fled from fornication.

This shows a right attitude in Joseph's heart. He didn't deal with this in some passive way, trying not to offend Potiphar's wife. Joseph didn't care about offending her. He was not going to let her compromise him, so he fled and left his garment in her hand.

Discern Love from Lust

And it came to pass, when she saw that he had left his garment in her hand, and was fled forth, that she called unto the men of her house, and spake unto them, saying, See, he hath brought in an Hebrew unto us to mock us; he came in unto me to lie with me, and I cried with a loud voice: and it came to pass, when he heard that I lifted up my voice and cried, that he left his garment with me, and fled, and got him out.

Genesis 39:13–15

This was a total lie on her part and illustrates something else. What this woman had for Joseph wasn't love. It was nothing but lust. And when she was rebuffed by Joseph, her so-called love turned into hatred instantly.

Sexual immorality is glorified and promoted in our society. We've been so sexualized today. It's just everywhere. And people may say they love someone, but it is not God's kind of love. It's just earthly, sensual, and devilish (James 3:15). You can tell that the "love" Potiphar's wife had for Joseph wasn't God's kind of love; it was all selfish. When she was rebuffed by Joseph, and he would not consent to having sexual relations, she lied about him and had Joseph committed unto prison. What kind of love is that? That's not love.

Sad to say, the world today doesn't have a clue about what God's kind of love is. The world's kind of love is emotional and selfish. And the moment self isn't satisfied, it turns into hatred. Potiphar's wife was willing to lie about Joseph and put him in prison. As far as she was concerned, he could have rotted in prison the rest of his days. Again, that's not love.

God's kind of love is described in 1 Corinthians 13:4–8, and it is vastly different than what the world today is calling love. What the world calls love is actually lust. One of the ways you can tell between God's kind of love and lust is selfishness. If it is God's kind of love, it will be unselfish. You will think about the other person more than about yourself. If it is lust, it's always about you. It's always about self-gratification.

Entrust Yourself to the Lord

And she laid up his garment by her, until his lord came home. And she spake unto him according to these words, saying, The Hebrew servant, which thou hast brought unto us, came in unto me to mock me: and it came to pass, as I lifted up my voice and cried, that he left his garment with me, and fled out. And it came to pass, when his master heard the words of his wife, which she spake unto him, saying, After this manner did thy servant to me; that his wrath was kindled. And Joseph's master took him, and put him into the prison, a place where the king's prisoners were bound: and he was there in the prison.

Genesis 39:16–20

One of the things to learn from this is what didn't happen. Joseph never tried to justify himself. Joseph's integrity did not let him sleep with his master's wife, and he could have found other servants who would have testified to his integrity, but he didn't. He didn't try to justify himself.

It's possible that, as a servant, Joseph didn't have the right to defend himself. His master may not have even asked him for his side of the story. But most people in a similar situation would have been shouting about our own innocence. We would be promoting ourselves, but Joseph just entrusted himself to the Lord.

In John 5:44, Jesus said,

How can ye believe, which receive honour one of another, and seek not the honour that cometh *from God only?*

Most of us are so dependent on being approved by people that we would sell our soul to the devil if it meant we were accepted by others. People who are truly in relationship with

God will stand before Him and not have to justify themselves. God will justify them.

Years ago, I was run out of town because I was falsely accused of doing some things, and it was not my fault. I missed a funeral that everybody was expecting me to go to. I should have been there, but I was actually kidnapped. That's the reason I didn't show up. But because I didn't show up, I had the members of five Bible studies I was leading just reject me. They didn't understand.

I could have justified myself, but I didn't want to reveal the people who kidnapped me and disgrace them while they were grieving over one of their relatives who had died. I just let it go. It was hard on Jamie and me, but we were more concerned about our relationship with God and our integrity rather than trying to justify ourselves. Five years later, God revealed what had happened and did it in a way that justified us.

I had another situation where a famous minister got up in front of their church, told their people I was the slickest cult leader since Jim Jones and encouraged them to burn my materials. Rather than retaliate, I just didn't say anything because I didn't want people to turn against this minister. I didn't know why they were so upset with me, but I also didn't try to justify myself.

About twenty years later, I was on a Christian television broadcast where we were both being interviewed. And this minister just told me how much they loved me and how they watched my program every day. They even invited me over to their house and gave me their personal phone number. I don't know what happened, but God put us back together. God defended me!

This is what you see here in Joseph's story. Joseph didn't defend himself. He trusted God to make it right.

Romans 12:19 says, *"Vengeance is mine; I will repay, saith the Lord."* You can just let God defend you instead of you defending yourself. If you have the attitude where you've always got to be right and correct every wrong, God can't defend you. You can either let God defend you or you can defend yourself. I can guarantee, God will defend you better than you could defend yourself.

Sometimes, you do need to stand up and fight against evil because it's truth against lies, but when it comes down to defending yourself, that's not a godly attitude. That's not the attitude that Joseph had. Joseph didn't say a thing. He knew the truth—and knew that his master's wife knew the truth—but even though he was being accused unjustly, he suffered the consequences. In spite of this injustice, he did not lose his faith in the two visions that God had given him about him being exalted and his brothers eventually coming and bowing down to him.

Chapter 6

Don't Look at Your Circumstances

But the LORD was with Joseph, and shewed him mercy, and gave him favour in the sight of the keeper of the prison. And the keeper of the prison committed to Joseph's hand all the prisoners that were *in the prison; and whatsoever they did there, he was the doer* of it. *The keeper of the prison looked not to any thing* that was *under his hand; because the LORD was with him, and* that *which he did, the LORD made* it *to prosper.*

Genesis 39:21–23

When it didn't look like Joseph was prosperous or that God was with him, the Scripture says, *"the LORD was with him"* (Gen. 39:3). And because of it, he was promoted and became head over his master's house. Then, Potiphar's wife lied about Joseph, and he was put into prison. Most people understand that was even worse than being a slave. I can guarantee you; Joseph's prison wasn't like our prisons today where they have flat-screen TVs and all sorts of other luxuries. This was a bad situation.

Yet, Scripture says, *"But the LORD was with Joseph, and shewed him mercy."* Here again, he is a prosperous man even in prison. That's awesome! It doesn't matter what things look like on the outside; you have to trust what God has revealed to you in your heart. Everything that's in the natural is subject to change.

In 2 Corinthians 4:17–18, the apostle Paul said,

> *For our light affliction, which is but for a moment, worketh for us a far more exceeding* and *eternal weight of glory; while we look not at the things which are seen, but at the things which are not seen: for the things which are seen* are *temporal; but the things which are not seen are eternal.*

Notice Paul says, *"the things which are seen are temporal."* That means they are temporary or subject to change. But the things that are not seen are eternal. Most people look at their life and evaluate things based on what they look like in the natural—what your doctor or bank account says. But you live your life by believing what God says instead.

My wife and I went through extreme poverty for ten years because of my own stupidity. There were times when Jamie was eight months pregnant, and we went for two weeks with nothing but water to drink. That's terrible. It was my fault because I thought that if I was called to the ministry I was sinning against God if I went and got a job. That was wrong, but that's the way I thought. My heart was right, and my head was wrong, but we never were poor in our hearts.

Even though we went through that poverty, we never talked or thought poor. We never saw that as the way our whole life was going to be. I never planned on staying in that situation. I still believed that God was for me, and I was going to prosper. It doesn't matter what your circumstances are like; it matters what you see in your heart, and I saw myself prospering. I wasn't prospering on the outside, but I was prospering on the inside.

There've been times that I've seen myself well when my body looked sick. I had a vision of me being healed. Proverbs 23:7 says, as a man *"thinketh in his heart, so is he."* If you can see yourself prosperous, regardless of what circumstances say, you will eventually be prosperous. If you can see yourself healed, you will eventually be healed. If you can see it on the inside— as you think in your heart—that's the way your life is going to be. Those are strong statements, but I learned to believe that from studying Joseph's life in the Bible.

The Lord was with Joseph and showed him mercy, even though in the natural, nobody would believe that. After God gave Joseph those two dreams (Gen. 37:5–11), everything in his life seemed to go in the wrong direction. His brothers rejected him, tried to kill him, and eventually sold him into slavery (Gen. 37:18–28). As a slave, his master's wife lied about him and had him thrown into prison (Gen. 39:13–20).

Every step Joseph took seemed to be headed downward, not upward. But those visions showed Joseph that someday he was going to be exalted, and his brothers would actually come and bow down to him.

Stay Encouraged

Some people might be able to last through a few negative things, but after years of things getting worse instead of better, most people would quit. Joseph maintained his integrity and his vision. When he was in prison, he wasn't complaining, he wasn't bitter, he wasn't angry, he wasn't depressed, and he wasn't giving up. He was still functioning—hitting on all cylinders—trusting God and believing that those visions were coming to pass.

Potiphar saw that the Lord was with Joseph, and that everything he did prospered. That doesn't happen to people who are bitter, angry, and operating in unforgiveness—people who have just given up and are depressed. No, Joseph was still believing God. He was still a man of integrity even though everything in his life looked like it was going wrong. And because he maintained a good attitude, the keeper of the prison put Joseph in charge of all the prisoners.

It doesn't say this specifically about the Egyptians, but when the Romans came along during the time of the New Testament (Acts 16: 23–24 and 27), if prisoners escaped, the jailer was put to death for letting them go. That means the keeper was totally responsible for what happened to those prisoners. I suspect the same thing applied in Egypt. But the keeper of the prison, regardless of the consequences, had so much trust in Joseph that he didn't even pay attention to what happened. He was basically just goofing off and enjoying himself because he trusted Joseph would do the right thing.

That is quite a statement about Joseph. There he was in prison, and yet Joseph was still seeking, trusting, and believing God. It was so evident that people saw it. And the keeper of the prison—at the hazard of his own life—was willing to just turn over all his responsibilities to Joseph.

At the time of this writing, I've got more than 1,100 people who work for me. The vast majority of them are just awesome, but we have a few people who are just depressed, discouraged, and have a bad attitude. I don't promote people like that. I wouldn't put them in charge of things. And I can guarantee you, it wasn't any different 4,000 years ago. For this jailer to put that kind of responsibility on Joseph is quite a testimony about the attitude Joseph had.

Joseph had not given up. He had not run up a white flag and thought, *What's the use? Serving God hasn't gotten me anywhere.* Joseph was still holding on to God even though every step he took looked like it was going in reverse instead of forward.

Serve with Excellence

And it came to pass after these things, that *the butler of the king of Egypt and* his *baker had offended their lord the king of Egypt. And Pharaoh was wroth against two of his officers, against the chief of the butlers, and against the chief of the bakers. And he put them in ward in the house of the captain of the guard, into the prison, the place where Joseph* was *bound. And the captain of the guard charged Joseph with them, and he served them: and they continued a season in ward.*

Genesis 40:1–4

This is providence that God put these two people in the same place Joseph was. God doesn't just force us into doing his will, but there is providence that works behind the scenes. If Joseph hadn't been sold into slavery and hadn't been put into prison, and if this baker and butler hadn't been put into prison, their connection would have never been made. Joseph would have never become the ruler over Egypt. I believe in the same way God is working on our behalf, even behind the scenes, when we don't even recognize it.

The person who ran the prison charged Joseph with the care of the butler and baker. They had been rejected by Pharaoh and put in prison. They came into the place where Joseph was a prisoner, and he was looking after them. Notice it says, *"he served them."* Here's Joseph in prison, operating in integrity, thinking of others and not just himself.

Most people in a similar situation would just sit in a corner, licking their wounds. They would be bitter and unforgiving. Most people would look at the butler and baker and think, *Well, who cares about them? Look at my situation!* But Joseph was serving people.

While imprisoned, Joseph ministered to people who were written off. They were prisoners, just like him, and they probably would have been thinking about themselves and their problems. But Joseph was serving them and ministering to them. As it turned out, the butler was his ticket out of prison.

Maybe you're in a situation right now where you have coworkers in need and you're only thinking about yourself and what's going on in your life. Yet, one of the quickest ways for you to get out of your problems is to minister to other people.

I'm saying this in love, but you might be bypassing the solution to your problems because you aren't thinking about anybody else but you. You may be sitting there, licking your wounds, and there are people God is bringing across your path who could transform your life. But you're missing opportunities because you're just looking at yourself.

I'm not condemning you. I want to encourage you. Look at what Joseph did! He was serving people in a situation where people should have been serving him. Somebody should have come and helped Joseph, and yet here he was just serving other people.

Your Eternal Reward

I heard a story about a couple who lived on a foreign mission field for decades. They had given their whole lives and ministered in obscurity to people who probably could never pay them back. Most people wouldn't have ever known about it.

When they grew old and retired, they turned the ministry over to somebody else and came home on a flight. As they were getting off the plane, they looked and saw people with banners saying, "Welcome Home!" The man thought to himself, *This is awesome! These people are here to welcome us home!* But it turned out those banners weren't for them. The crowd was there to welcome some dignitary on the plane, but there wasn't anybody at the airport to welcome the missionary couple.

The man started complaining and told his wife, "We've given our life for decades. We've served, and there wasn't one single person here to greet us. There's a person who's just a celebrity, who hasn't done anything to change a person's life, and they had all these people there to welcome them home."

His wife grabbed him by the hand and said, "But we aren't home yet!" That's awesome!

In this life, you may never get the recognition you deserve, but you aren't home yet. This world isn't our home. Someday, we're going to stand before God, and I guarantee you, those who have led other people to the Lord and served God are going shine like the sun. There are rewards for you that are out of this world, but you cannot just be thinking about yourself in this life.

Even if Joseph's situation had never improved, when he died and went into eternity, God would have rewarded him for the way he was serving other people in a terrible situation. When he was in trouble himself, rather than thinking about all his own problems, he was ministering to other people. No action like that will go unrewarded someday. In Matthew 10:41–42, Jesus said,

> *He that receiveth a prophet in the name of a prophet shall receive a prophet's reward; and he that receiveth a righteous man in the name of a righteous man shall receive a righteous man's reward. And whosoever shall give to drink unto one of these little ones a cup of cold* water *only in the name of a disciple, verily I say unto you, he shall in no wise lose his reward.*

God pays attention to the smallest thing. So, whether it looks like you're ever going to come out of your situation or not, you need to start thinking about somebody else. You need to start serving other people.

Show Concern for Others

And they dreamed a dream both of them, each man his dream in one night, each man according to the interpretation of his dream, the butler and the baker of the king of Egypt, which were bound in the prison. And Joseph came in unto them in the morning, and looked upon them, and, behold, they were sad. And he asked Pharaoh's officers that were with him in the ward of his lord's house, saying, Wherefore look ye so sadly to day?

Genesis 40:5–7

This is amazing! These guys were in prison, and back in those days it wasn't like it is today, where they have air conditioning and heating, and prisoners are fed three meals a day in sanitary conditions. Prison back in ancient times was terrible, but Joseph considered it unusual for the butler and baker to be sad.

Most people would think, *Well, everybody in prison is sad.* But that wasn't the case for people in Joseph's prison because he ministered to them. Joseph treated these people kindly. They were probably being treated better in prison than they had ever been treated in their lives, so much so that when he came in and found the prisoners feeling sad, it was unusual.

This says volumes about Joseph and what kind of a person he was. He was making the lives of everybody around him better because he wasn't sitting there griping and complaining about his own situation. We live in a fallen world, and bad things happen. So, you may be suffering, but you don't have to let that dictate your response. You can choose to still rejoice in the Lord, regardless of what's going on. Philippians 4:4 says,

Rejoice in the Lord alway: and again I say, Rejoice.

Paul was the one who was commanding that, and he had been in prison.

In Acts 16:23–28, Paul and Silas were in the lowest dungeon in the prison. Their backs were beaten, and their feet and their hands were in the stocks. Even though there was no light in that dungeon, and there were all sorts of other things going on, they were praising God at midnight. And they weren't praising God to get something, because when the earthquake came, all their chains fell off, the prison doors opened, and they didn't leave—they stayed. They were praising God because they really loved Him. And the prisoners who heard them didn't leave either.

Paul and Silas were showing so much joy and worship toward God that the other prisoners were experiencing more freedom in prison than they ever had on the outside, so much so that when their chains fell off and their doors were opened, they didn't leave. That's what Paul and Silas told the Philippian jailer who was threatening to take his own life—*"Do thyself no harm: for we are all here"* (Acts 16:28).

In a similar way, Joseph was in prison, thinking of other people and ministering to them. Perhaps your situation isn't nearly as bad as Joseph's, and yet you're just thinking about yourself. You're not ministering to anybody else because you think you're hurting so badly. Holding on to your bitterness, unforgiveness, and anger is like drinking poison and expecting another person to be hurt. But they're going on with their lives while you're the one who's hurting yourself. You need to get over it and start thinking about other people.

Joseph was ministering to other prisoners so much that when they were sad, it was unusual. Joseph was a person who had humbled himself. He was putting God first and other people ahead of himself. Joseph was holding onto the vision that God had given him through those two dreams, and he knew that he was going to get past all of this someday. He was not giving up.

God Reveals Secrets

And they said unto him, We have dreamed a dream, and there is no interpreter of it. And Joseph said unto them, Do not interpretations belong to God? tell me them, I pray you.

Genesis 40:8

Joseph had an anointing for interpreting dreams. He'd not only had his two dreams (Gen. 37:5–11), but here he interprets two dreams for the butler and baker. He basically says, "God is the one who reveals secrets, so tell me your dreams."

And the chief butler told his dream to Joseph, and said to him, In my dream, behold, a vine was before me; and in the vine were three branches: and it was as though it budded, and her blossoms shot forth; and the clusters thereof brought forth ripe grapes: and Pharaoh's cup was in my hand: and I took the grapes, and pressed them into Pharaoh's cup, and I gave the cup into Pharaoh's hand. And Joseph said unto him, This is the interpretation of it: The three branches are three days: yet within three days shall Pharaoh lift up thine head, and restore thee unto thy place: and thou shalt deliver Pharaoh's cup into his hand, after the former manner when thou wast his butler.

Genesis 40:9–13

This is amazing to me. I'm not sure that I would have gotten out of this dream what Joseph did, but this was the anointing of God on him. Joseph immediately interpreted the dream and then asked,

But think on me when it shall be well with thee, and shew kindness, I pray thee, unto me, and make mention of me unto Pharaoh, and bring me out of this house: for

indeed I was stolen away out of the land of the Hebrews: and here also have I done nothing that they should put me into the dungeon.

Genesis 40:14–15

This is the only thing that could ever be construed as Joseph lamenting his situation. When the butler was restored to his position, Joseph just asked to be remembered and to put in a good word with Pharaoh. I don't believe it is necessarily an indication that Joseph was bitter or hurt because that would be so contrary to his whole life. But it does show that he was planning to come out of there. He was not resigned to just staying in prison the rest of his life. He was seeing past these things, and he asked the butler to remember him when he was restored back to his position.

Not Withholding the Truth

When the chief baker saw that the interpretation was good, he said unto Joseph, I also was in my dream, and, behold, I had three white baskets on my head: and in the uppermost basket there was of all manner of bakemeats for Pharaoh; and the birds did eat them out of the basket upon my head. And Joseph answered and said, This is the interpretation thereof: The three baskets are three days: yet within three days shall Pharaoh lift up thy head from off

*thee, and shall hang thee on a tree; and the birds shall eat
thy flesh from off thee.*

Genesis 40:16–19

Since the interpretation of the butler's dream had a good
outcome, the baker thought he'd share his dream too. But
instead, it was terrible. In three days, the baker was going to
have his head cut off and his body hung on a tree so the birds
could eat his flesh.

Again, this says a lot about Joseph and the amount of
integrity he had. There are a lot of ministers today who will
say whatever it takes to tickle people's ears and to get a positive
response. Joseph was ministering to these people and had a
desire to be a blessing. But at the same time, he was a greater
servant to God. Whatever God said was what Joseph was
going to say.

There are a lot of ministers today who will not stand up
and proclaim the truth and tell people that living in sin opens a
door to the devil. The devil only comes to steal, kill, and destroy
(John 10:10). But because some minister thinks, *Well, that'll
drive people away*, they won't share the truth. Joseph could have
thought that way, but instead he was bold enough to say exactly
what God revealed to him.

I had a friend of mine who was a real demonstrative person. He would scream, yell, spit on people, and do all kinds of

things. (By comparison, I'm really tame!) One time, he was ministering in Russia and shouting, "Praise the Lord!" But his interpreter was just calmly saying, *"Slava bogu."* So, this minister shouted, "Praise the Lord," again, and the interpreter just said, *"Slava bogu,"* without showing any emotion.

Finally, this minister turned to his interpreter and said, "You're supposed to be interpreting for me! You say it like I say it!" And as soon as he said that to the interpreter, the Lord spoke to that minister and said, "You're supposed to be interpreting for Me. It's not up to you to say what you want to say; you are supposed to be hearing from Me and telling people what I say."

Joseph was not a man pleaser. He was listening to God. There's a lesson to be learned here. There are so many ministers today who, if God showed them something and commanded them to rebuke somebody, they would not do it. They just minister to try and make everybody feel good. But we are not supposed to be interpreting for ourselves. We are not supposed to be speaking on our own behalf. We're supposed to be interpreting from God. I guarantee you, there are things in our society today that we need to be talking against.

The Lord says, emphatically, *"The thief* [Satan] *cometh not, but for to steal, and to kill, and to destroy"* (John 10:10a), and *"Know ye not, that to whom ye yield yourselves servants to obey, his servants ye are to whom ye obey; whether of sin unto death, or of obedience unto righteousness?"* (Rom. 6:16). Yet, there are a lot of ministers who won't stand up today and say those things. They're interpreting for themselves. They're saying what they think will make the people come and give money instead of speaking the truth. But it's the truth that sets people free (John 8:32).

So, Joseph honored God by telling the truth even when it looked like it was against someone. Joseph was a faithful man.

Still Standing Strong

And he restored the chief butler unto his butlership again; and he gave the cup into Pharaoh's hand: but he hanged the chief baker: as Joseph had interpreted to them. Yet did not the chief butler remember Joseph, but forgat him.

Genesis 40:21–23

This is miraculous! Joseph prophesied things that weren't general. This was so specific. The interpretations had to either be totally from God or Joseph would have had to totally miss it—but no, they were from God.

Now, you would think that after something like this, a guy would remember who Joseph was and what he had done. The butler had been in prison and could have stayed there until he rotted. Yet, Joseph interpreted his dream, and he was promoted. It came to pass exactly as Joseph said, but the chief butler just forgot him. It didn't say the chief butler was afraid to mention Joseph or afraid that it might not have been received. The Scripture said he just totally forgot Joseph. He wasn't appreciated at all.

There are so many times that we do something for somebody, and they don't appreciate it. Most people would feel sorry for themselves, thinking about how bad things are. That did not stop Joseph from still seeking the Lord. For two years, Joseph was forgotten. He had withstood the rejection of his brothers, was sold into slavery, was falsely accused, and put into prison. What if all those things had happened to you, but then you helped somebody, and they just totally forgot about you? Most people wouldn't have been able to survive that, but Joseph just kept standing even after all of those things.

In Genesis 41, we'll see where Joseph is finally promoted. But it wasn't until thirteen years after his first dreams. So, for thirteen years, everything in Joseph's life was going in the wrong direction. Some people can't stand for thirteen weeks or even thirteen days. Joseph went thirteen years without one positive thing happening, and yet he stood strong. If Joseph could do that without being born again, without the baptism of the Holy Spirit, then we should do no less.

Chapter 7

Keep Going and Don't Quit

And it came to pass at the end of two full years, that Pharaoh dreamed.

Genesis 41:1a

The butler received a good report from Joseph, was restored to his position serving Pharaoh, and yet he didn't remember Joseph. Joseph had even asked him, "Remember me when you come before Pharaoh, and tell him that I was put here unjustly," but the butler totally forgot for two whole years. It wasn't that he was afraid to speak up, he had just forgotten Joseph. I'll tell you though, Joseph shows us it's not really over until it's over. His story wasn't finished, and he remained faithful instead of becoming bitter.

The Holy Spirit has used these truths about Joseph to encourage me, and I praise God that I didn't quit on what He called me to do. During the first ten years of my ministry, there was very little evidence that God's blessing was on it. In my heart, I felt like I was anointed and blessed of God, but in the natural it was making very little impact.

Early on in my ministry, I went to a conference at Calvary Cathedral in Fort Worth, Texas, where Bob Nichols was the pastor. I really appreciate Pastor Bob. He is a great friend of mine today. But back then, I had only met him once previously, and it was not a positive experience. That was the only contact I had with Pastor Bob before going to his church for that conference. I thought that if he ever heard my name again, he'd probably turn and run in the opposite direction.

All of the big-name ministers at the time were there, and they were prophesying to each other, getting all kinds of awesome words from the Lord. I remember sitting in that huge auditorium full of people, right in the middle of my row, about ten seats in from the aisle. I felt so small and insignificant. During the song service, they said, "Go around and greet someone," but that whole time, I was thinking, *God, I need help. I need somebody to encourage me.*

Right about then, Pastor Bob somehow saw me in a crowd of two thousand people. He got off the platform and ran back to where I was in the middle of my row. Pastor Bob excused himself, pushed his way through all of those people and just started hugging me. It wasn't just one of those little charismatic hugs, either. He wrapped his arms around me and wouldn't let go. Pastor Bob started saying, "Brother, I love you, and God loves you. Don't quit! Hold on!" He just held on to me and ministered to me. Then, he went back up to the front of the auditorium.

That encouraged me. It blessed me to think that this well-known man who was hosting this big conference had singled me out. He didn't have to do that. I took it as an expression of God's love, and it really ministered to me. He saw something in me that only God could see. I had this vision of touching the whole world with the Gospel, but here I was feeling small and insignificant. What Pastor Bob did lit a fire under me, and I was able to hold on to that vision.

All these years later, through our television ministry and Charis Bible College, we are taking the Gospel farther and deeper than ever before. We have schools all around the world and billions of people can watch our program at any time. As a matter of fact, Pastor Bob has faithfully served on my board of directors and has had a front-row seat to watch what God is doing through this ministry. That's awesome!

One of the reasons I stood all those years was because of the example of Joseph. I saw that Joseph had a vision. He held on and didn't quit. His example has kept me going, and I thank the Lord that I didn't give up on the vision God had for me.

Interpreting Dreams from God

And it came to pass at the end of two full years, that Pharaoh dreamed; and behold, he stood by the river. And, behold, there came up out of the river seven well favoured kine and fatfleshed; and they fed in a meadow. And, behold, seven other kine came up after them out of the river, ill favoured and leanfleshed; and stood by the other kine upon the brink of the river. And the ill favoured and leanfleshed kine did eat up the seven well favoured and fat kine. So Pharaoh awoke. And he slept and dreamed the second time: and, behold, seven ears of corn came up upon one stalk, rank and good. And, behold, seven thin ears and blasted with the east wind sprung up after them. And the seven thin ears devoured the seven rank and full ears. And Pharaoh awoke, and, behold, it was a dream.

Genesis 41:1–7

Pharaoh knew in his spirit that there was significance to these dreams, but his mind couldn't figure it out. This illustrates how we can know things by our spirits that don't make sense to our minds. Pharaoh knew that these dreams were supernatural, and something was being spoken to him. Just as with the dreams of the butler and baker in Genesis 40, God used natural things to give supernatural revelation.

And it came to pass in the morning that his spirit was troubled; and he sent and called for all the magicians of Egypt, and all the wise men thereof: and Pharaoh told them his dream; but there was none that could interpret them unto Pharaoh.

Genesis 41:8

Pharaoh was looking for an interpretation to his dreams. He knew these dreams were significant, but he just didn't know how to interpret them. So, he called for all the wise men and magicians, but no one in his court could interpret it.

In the same way that the Lord can make blind eyes see, He can also make seeing eyes and hearts blind. Pharaoh's wise men, who followed false gods, could not interpret the dream given to him by the one true living God. Joseph, as we've seen, was anointed to interpret dreams and he had confidence in God, despite everything in the natural that indicated otherwise. He had received two dreams from God that showed his family would bow before him someday (Gen. 37:1–5), and he correctly interpreted the dreams of Pharaoh's butler and baker (Gen. 40:5–22). It was supernatural the way God made things work together so that only Joseph was in a position to interpret Pharaoh's dreams. This was all planned by the Lord.

Overcome People's Opinions

Then spake the chief butler unto Pharaoh, saying, I do remember my faults this day: Pharaoh was wroth with his servants, and put me in ward in the captain of the guard's house, both *me and the chief baker: and we dreamed a dream in one night, I and he; we dreamed each man according to the interpretation of his dream. And* there was *there with us a young man, an Hebrew, servant to the captain of the guard; and we told him, and he interpreted to us our dreams; to each man according to his dream he did interpret. And it came to pass, as he interpreted to us, so it was; me he restored unto mine office, and him he hanged.*

Genesis 41:9–13

This is the man who had been in prison and had Joseph interpret his dream. After it came to pass, he finally remembered Joseph two years later. Pharaoh was looking for an interpretation of his dreams, and the butler told him there is someone who could do it—but he was a Hebrew.

There are a number of scriptures that show how Egyptians hated Hebrews (Gen. 43:32 and 46:33–34; Ex. 1:12 and 8:25–26; and Ps. 105:23–25). Later, when Joseph brought his father and his brothers down into Egypt, they settled in the land of Goshen because Hebrews were herders (Gen. 46:28–34)—they were considered inferior. There was a prejudice against them, and they couldn't dwell with the Egyptians.

Then Pharaoh sent and called Joseph, and they brought him hastily out of the dungeon: and he shaved himself, and changed his raiment, and came in unto Pharaoh.

Genesis 41:14

Pharaoh called for someone who was in a dungeon and was despised by his people—a person who was a prisoner and a Hebrew. Most people in prison are there because they've done something wrong. In addition to that, Egyptians were prejudiced against Hebrews. And yet, here's Pharaoh—who had nowhere else to turn—willing to call on a person who was disesteemed, prejudiced against by the Egyptians, and sitting in prison.

It's amazing to me that the most important man in the strongest nation on the face of the earth submitted himself and asked for help from a person in Joseph's position. I believe it had to be God's influence because this sort of thing wouldn't just happen normally.

It doesn't matter what other people say about you. It doesn't matter what circumstances say about you. It's what you think in your heart. Joseph had a vision for his life, which is why he didn't get discouraged when he was sold into slavery (Gen. 37:26–28) or defend himself when he was falsely accused by Potiphar's wife and cast into prison (Gen. 39:7–20). He just kept serving with excellence because he knew that slavery and prison were not the end of his story. He trusted God.

Honor Authority

It may seem like a small thing that Joseph shaved and changed his clothes, but I believe that this speaks to the excellence that was in Joseph. Egyptians were clean shaven, so Joseph made himself the same before he came in to meet with

Pharaoh. In other words, he dressed for success. Now, I don't believe that you have to wear three-piece suits and ties all the time, but at the same time, I believe our society has just gotten so sloppy.

There was a man who came into our office one time as I was walking around and greeting my staff. He was wearing an old t-shirt that was out of shape, shorts, and flip flops. He hadn't combed his hair, and he smelled bad. He looked like he had just come off the street. As he passed, I said hello to him and watched as he went into my IT guy's office. Later in the day, I asked my staff member what that man had come in for, and I learned he was applying for a job. I said, "Don't hire him!" He tried to tell me about this man's qualifications, but I said, "I don't care what his qualifications are. I don't want somebody like that working here. If that's the way he comes in when he is looking for work, what's he going to be like once we hire him?"

Some people reading this may be thinking, *That's prejudiced! You're judging a person based on their appearance.* Well, to a degree, I was. A person's appearance is a reflection of who they are. It's not a perfect reflection, but it does say something about a person's attitude.

Years ago, my youngest son got his nose pierced, his ears pierced, his eyebrow pierced, and his lip pierced—and I just didn't like it. I didn't criticize or reject him over it, but I said, "People are going to judge you based on the way you look." He didn't agree with what I had to say, but when he went to get a job, he took all these piercings out and changed some things. People won't hire you—at least not for a good job—looking like that. Now, he might've gotten a job as a pin cushion looking like that, but if he wanted to have something more than that, he had to adjust and meet society's expectations.

I'm telling you these things because Joseph respected Pharoah's office and wanted to meet his expectations. That was a reflection of Joseph. He was a person of excellence.

In Daniel 6:3, Darius thought to promote Daniel over the entire kingdom because he had an excellent spirit. Excellence is something people notice. You can get into a ditch by being a perfectionist and being critical of others if everything isn't exactly as you say. That's not what I'm talking about. But I am talking about presenting yourself the best you can.

Some of us look better than others. I have never been accused of being the best-looking guy around, but I can at least comb my hair, brush my teeth, and do the best I can with what I've got. There are some people who don't care how they dress or how they look. A person's appearance says something about them.

Joseph, when he knew that he was going before the most powerful man on the earth at that time, dressed accordingly. It is a small thing, but the way you look projects an image—not only in how you dress but also your attitude.

Proverbs 31:25–26 talks about the virtuous woman, adorning herself with wisdom. There are women that wouldn't dare leave home without their hair being fixed, without their makeup on, or without all their jewelry. But they'll leave home with a bad attitude, and that is much worse than having on the wrong clothes. So, this isn't only talking about the clothes that you wear but the way you project yourself.

I was watching a movie one time, and it had some scenes where the people were sad, and they just looked ugly. But then they started laughing and smiling, it changed everything. I'll tell you, a smile looks good on anybody. When you're ministering to other people, you ought to smile every once in a while. You ought to go out of your way to do something to change things and build people up. A small thing that can have a big impact is how you present yourself.

J.C. Penney founded the department store chain that bears his name. It's been said that when he went to hire for a management position, he would take the person out to eat and watch them. If the person salted their food before they tasted it, he wouldn't hire them. It showed that a person was just a creature of habit. They didn't taste the food first to see if it was already salted and seasoned properly. They just did things out of habit. J.C. Penney wanted people who would think and react to situations instead of just going through the motions. Some people may not think that's fair, but he built one of the largest retail store chains in the history of the world. It was because there were little things that he paid attention to.

If you are going to truly prosper, you cannot just wait until something big comes along and then do it right. You've got to start doing what's right when it's something small. You've got to start being faithful in that which is least before the things that are bigger will be committed unto you. I think that this is important.

Joseph didn't just go to Pharaoh's palace with his prison garments on. He put on nice clothes and shaved before he came before Pharaoh. That says something. He presented himself with excellence because he held on to that vision from God—that he would not be a slave and prisoner forever. It goes to show that if you believe in God, you'll win if you just don't quit.

Chapter 8

Make Yourself Usable

And Pharaoh said unto Joseph, I have dreamed a dream, and there is *none that can interpret it: and I have heard say of thee,* that *thou canst understand a dream to interpret it. And Joseph answered Pharaoh, saying,* It is *not in me: God shall give Pharaoh an answer of peace.*

Genesis 41:15–16

One of the reasons God used Joseph and promoted him is because he didn't take credit for himself; he gave the glory to God. He didn't point Pharaoh to himself; he pointed Pharaoh to God.

Isaiah 42:8 says, *"My glory will I not give to another."* The previous verses talk about Jesus, the Messiah; and God the Father said, "I am not going to give my glory to anybody but Jesus." The moment you start trying to take credit and receive glory for what God is doing through you, it will shut off the flow of God's power and anointing.

This is one reason I believe it took thirteen years from the time God gave Joseph those dreams until he stood before

Pharaoh. People don't just come immediately to a place to where they promote God over themselves. You don't reach a place of humility and submission like that overnight. That's against human nature.

When I first got started in ministry, I used to spend hours praying, "Oh God, please use me!" But one day, the Lord spoke to me and said, "The reason I don't use you is because you aren't usable. Quit praying, 'God use me,' and pray, 'God make me usable..'" So, that's what I started doing.

It took years, but God has blessed me and opened doors. We have the potential to reach over five billion people per day through television. We're reaching people all over the world, but it took a period of time to get to that place. If thirty, forty, or fifty years ago, God would have given me the responsibility and the opportunities I have now, I would have blown the whole thing.

When I first arrived in Vietnam while serving in the army, I was studying the Bible and read about the parable of the mustard seed.

And he said, Whereunto shall we liken the kingdom of God? or with what comparison shall we compare it? It is like a grain of mustard seed, which, when it is sown in the earth, is less than all the seeds that be in the earth: but when it is sown, it groweth up, and becometh greater

*than all herbs, and shooteth out great branches; so that the
fowls of the air may lodge under the shadow of it.*

Mark 4:30–32

I saw in this parable that the Lord was talking about growth, comparing the kingdom of God to a huge tree that spreads out until the birds of the air come and land in it. Jesus was saying that God sows a seed in your heart, and it grows. As it begins to produce, you become usable and begin ministering to other people, and their lives are changed.

As I was reading this, I prayed, "God, this is what I want. I want you to touch my life and use me so I can touch people all over the world." I had no idea I'd be touching millions of people around the world through television and Charis Bible College, but I had the desire for it. So, I was just praying, "God, I want to be this huge tree that reaches out to touch and bless people."

And the Lord spoke to me and said, "If I were to answer your prayer today and give you this worldwide ministry that you desire, the first bird that landed on one of your branches would cause the whole thing to fall over, because your root is about an inch deep." I wanted to be used, but I just wasn't usable yet. I had to be faithful with the small things I was assigned to, become rooted in God's Word, and continue to grow.

It takes time to mature and get to a place where you give God the glory, but this is really a revelation right here when Joseph says, "It is *not in me: God shall give Pharaoh an answer of peace*" (Gen. 41:16). Joseph had learned humility and submission. He had learned to give God the credit. He had learned that if there was any good thing in him, it was because of God.

I'll tell you, the very reason that some people haven't been promoted from the pit to the palace is because God can't trust them with it. Success is a greater temptation than hardship. Now, to many people, that won't ring true, but it is.

If you have any commitment to the Lord at all, when you're in a desperate situation what else can you do but trust God? It's one thing to say that Joseph continued to trust God when he was sold into slavery, but what other options did he have? Once he went from being a rich kid, the favorite son of his father, to being a slave in a foreign land, what other hope did he have? When Joseph was put into prison, and it looked like there was no way out of prison except feet first, what else could he do? Joseph had to hang onto God.

But once you get promoted to a place of authority, there is a greater temptation for you to think, *I don't have to trust God now that everything in my life's going good.* More people have been destroyed by prosperity than have ever been destroyed by hardship. I know that there are people who would disagree with that, and you're entitled to your opinion, but I'm not going to agree with you or we'd both be wrong. I'm telling you, this is true! You have to humble yourself to be usable.

Prepare for the Moment

And Pharaoh said unto Joseph, In my dream, behold, I stood upon the bank of the river: and, behold, there came up out of the river seven kine, fatfleshed and well favoured; and they fed in a meadow: and, behold, seven other kine came up after them, poor and very ill favoured and leanfleshed, such as I never saw in all the land of Egypt for badness: and the lean and the ill favoured kine did eat up the first seven fat kine: and when they had eaten them up, it could not be known that they had eaten them; but they were *still ill favoured, as at the beginning. So I awoke. And I saw in my dream, and, behold, seven ears came up in one stalk, full and good: and, behold, seven ears, withered, thin,* and *blasted with the east wind, sprung up after them: and the thin ears devoured the seven good ears: and I told* this *unto the magicians; but* there *was none that could declare* it *to me.*

Genesis 41:17–24

When Pharaoh recounted this to Joseph, he added a little bit and said he had never seen cattle that were as ill-favored as these. He didn't say that when he first shared his dreams with all of his staff, but when Pharaoh talked to Joseph, he expounded and said they were the worst cattle he had ever seen. The world likes to exaggerate and present worst-case scenarios because bad news gets people's attention. It was clear this was something that really troubled Pharaoh and he wanted an answer right away; he was putting pressure on Joseph.

One of the reasons people fold under pressure is because they wait until the "big" situations to believe God. If they have not learned to trust God in the small things, they will not be able to trust Him in the big things.

When David fought Goliath, everyone mocked him because of his belief that he could win. Goliath was a giant, the champion of the Philistines (1 Sam. 17:4), and David was only a boy. But David said something really important:

> *And David said unto* [King] *Saul, Thy servant kept his father's sheep, and there came a lion, and a bear, and took a lamb out of the flock: and I went out after him, and smote him, and delivered* it *out of his mouth: and when he arose against me, I caught* him *by his beard, and smote him, and slew him. Thy servant slew both the lion and the bear: and this uncircumcised Philistine shall be as one of them, seeing he hath defied the armies of the living God. David said moreover, The* LORD *that delivered me out of the paw of the lion, and out of the paw of the bear, he will deliver me out of the hand of this Philistine. And Saul said unto David, Go, and the* LORD *be with thee.*

1 Samuel 17:34–37

David revealed that this was not the first time he had depended on God for a victory against something bigger than himself. Before facing Goliath, he had killed a lion and a bear with his bare hands. He knew he could defeat Goliath with God's help.

Joseph had a vision from God, and the Lord had shown him favor through all those years in slavery and prison. Even though it appeared every step he took was downward, Joseph still trusted God.

Even though it doesn't appear Joseph had any lag time between Pharoah's request and his response, he didn't have to think about his answer. Like David, Joseph had been preparing for his moment for years. He was focused on God and the anointing was there.

And Joseph said unto Pharaoh, The dream of Pharaoh is one: God hath shewed Pharaoh what he is about to do.

Genesis 41:25

Consistency Is the Key

All of us would like to just have the answer and know exactly what to do in a crisis situation, but the sad fact is most people don't seek the Lord until they're in that crisis situation. Joseph had been faithful to the Lord for thirteen years and because of it, his heart was prepared. Everything that happened up to that point was a crescendo. This was the climax his life was headed toward, so he was ready.

Are you going to be ready when God opens an opportunity for you? When people are in a crisis, they get serious; they spend time fasting and believing God for something. But really, that's not the right way to do it. That's better than not seeking God at all, but the right way is to seek God with your whole heart *all* of the time. Even if it takes you thirteen years of seeking God, when you get to that moment, you will have everything you need to be able to deal with it and to succeed in that situation.

This is one of the lessons we can learn from Joseph. He was consistent, and that made him usable. The fact that Pharaoh gave these dreams and Joseph was ready to answer was because he had been preparing himself. Preparation time is never wasted. This is what we tell our Charis Bible College students all the time. Many of them have a dream to go out and do something. They're called to ministry, business, politics, or something else, and they have a dream. But they come to Bible college, and they sometimes don't appreciate the time they are spending. They're wanting to get on with what God has called them to do, but we tell them preparation time is never wasted time.

This is why first-year students in my class at Charis are required to read through the Bible during the school year. In fact, it is 20 percent of their course grade. I think people who come to Bible college should actually read the Bible, amen! And part of the reason we require it is because they need to spend time getting rooted in God's Word.

It's just like the parable of the mustard seed. They want to spread their branches and reach the world for Jesus, but the first bit of adversity and persecution that comes their way will knock them over like a gust of wind if they haven't spent time rooting themselves in the Word and growing in their personal relationship with God. You will be more effective if you prepare your heart for when the right time comes. This is what Joseph did, and he had an answer for Pharaoh.

Knowing Things to Come

The seven good kine are *seven years; and the seven good ears* are *seven years: the dream* is *one. And the seven thin and ill favoured kine that came up after them* are *seven years; and the seven empty ears blasted with the east wind shall be seven years of famine. This* is *the thing which I have spoken unto Pharaoh: What God is about to do he sheweth unto Pharaoh.*

Genesis 41:26–28

God created all of us, and the Holy Spirit will show us things to come (John 16:13). I believe that before any negative circumstance comes into your life, if you are in tune with God,

He will show you and prepare you for it. I really believe that. Now, that is not to say every time something bad happens it doesn't catch people by surprise. It happens all the time. But that's because people aren't always in tune with the Lord.

I believe that God will show us things. God will even make the provision before a problem exists. God provided the seven years of abundance before there were seven years of famine. There were not seven years of famine first. No, God made a provision before the problem arose.

God provides for us, and everything we need is available; but we have to be sensitive enough to know it. Any time you have a situation develop, you just need to have the mindset that God was not caught by surprise. He knew what was coming. That doesn't mean God caused it, but He did know problems would come. If cancer tries to come on you, God knew it was going to happen. If you were in tune with Him, you would be prepared and ready to deal with it. God has made the provision—the supply—available before the need ever existed.

Sad to say, so many people just go through life doing their own thing, not seeking God. When they get a cancer diagnosis, all of a sudden, their world comes crashing in. That's when they go to seeking God with their whole heart. It's better to seek God in a crisis situation than not to seek Him at all, but when you are seeking Him all along and having your heart prepared, then you could just get to a place to where it's no big deal. You can say, "God heals cancer; and if for some reason, I don't get better, I'm going to be with Jesus. It's going to be awesome!" You can get to a place where nothing surprises you and where you aren't afraid of an evil report coming in the future.

I'd like to think that's the way all Christians are, but I deal with a lot of people, and I know that is rare. The vast majority of Christians only seek God when their backs are against the wall and when they're in a crisis situation. And that's exactly the reason they have so many crisis situations!

I'm telling you, we need to be like Joseph, who sought God and was ready. When the time came, he was up to the task because he had been preparing for it his entire life. Nothing is going to catch God by surprise, and if you would just stay in tune with Him, nothing will catch you by surprise either.

Interpreting Dreams

Behold, there come seven years of great plenty throughout all the land of Egypt: and there shall arise after them seven years of famine; and all the plenty shall be forgotten in the land of Egypt; and the famine shall consume the land. and the plenty shall not be known in the land by reason of that famine following; for it shall be *very grievous. And for that the dream was doubled unto Pharaoh twice;* it is *because the thing* is *established by God, and God will shortly bring it to pass.*

Genesis 41:29–32

113

Joseph had two dreams (Gen. 37:5–11). They were both saying the same thing, but it was said in two separate dreams. Joseph tells Pharaoh any time that a dream is doubled—two dreams saying the same thing—it's because the thing is established, and it cannot be changed.

Now, I believe there are dreams that have nothing to do with God. There are dreams where something weird is happening (like joining the Air Force to pay off your ministry debts), and those don't amount to anything. But then there are dreams that come from God.

Sometimes, a dream from God is about something that's not established, and it's God showing you what will happen if you don't change. It could be a warning, telling you to make changes in your life or take evasive actions so you can change what the dream depicted. But once a God-given dream is doubled unto you, and it has the same meaning, that means that the thing is established and cannot be changed.

This is a powerful passage of scripture, especially for anybody who believes that God will speak to you through dreams. If you want to interpret dreams, this is a key: once a dream is doubled unto you and the same message is given in different dreams, it's established and will shortly come to pass! But the dreams have to be from God.

Chapter 9

Know Your True Identity

Now therefore let Pharaoh look out a man discreet and wise, and set him over the land of Egypt. Let Pharaoh do this, and let him appoint officers over the land, and take up the fifth part of the land of Egypt in the seven plenteous years. And let them gather all the food of those good years that come, and lay up corn under the hand of Pharaoh, and let them keep food in the cities. And that food shall be for store to the land against the seven years of famine, which shall be in the land of Egypt; that the land perish not through the famine.

Genesis 41:33–36

Here's Joseph speaking to Pharaoh. He's heard the dreams, given the interpretation, and telling Pharaoh what he needs to do. To me, this is amazing! This was a guy who was in prison, talking to the most powerful man on the planet—a prisoner telling Pharaoh how to respond. Not only that, but Joseph was also considered beneath the Egyptians. They didn't like Hebrews at all! But there he was telling Pharaoh what to do.

It is amazing the favor God will give you if you seek Him with all of your heart. God was with Joseph, and he had favor in the sight of Potiphar (Gen. 39:3–4) and the keeper of the prison (Gen. 39:21). And then he has favor in the sight of Pharaoh, the most powerful man on the planet. There's no way that could happen in the natural. It wasn't because he was a prisoner, and it wasn't because he was a Hebrew; it was because he was anointed by God.

I'll tell you, we undersell things like this. I don't think we fully understand them sometimes. We often look at things through the eyes of unbelievers and we see ourselves as nothing. But you need to see yourself as a powerful and anointed person, because God is with you.

A friend of mine, Rich Van Winkle, wrote a book on identity called, *As He Is . . . So Are We.* On the cover is a picture of a man looking at himself in the mirror. You see the side of the man's face, so you can tell that it's a person standing there, but the image in the mirror is of Jesus. I think that's awesome! This is the way we need to see ourselves—not in the way the mirror looks in the natural, but who we are in Christ. In the natural, I may not look like much, but in my spirit, I am absolutely awesome. I am anointed by God, and so are you! You've got to be able to see yourself this way.

Joseph was a man who was considered below the Egyptians and who was a prisoner just a few moments before, but then he gives Pharaoh direction about what he needed to do. Only God could promote someone like that, and only a humble person could take that position. Joseph was in a position where, if God didn't intervene and back him up, Pharaoh could take great offense by having a prisoner telling him what to do. Pharaoh could have gotten mad and had Joseph killed.

Joseph put himself on the line, but he had confidence. He knew God called him. He knew God promoted him. You have to be sensitive enough to the Lord to be able to take advantage of an opportunity when it comes. There are some people who are just so tentative and fearful of making a mistake, they would never step out and do something like Joseph did. But Joseph was confident in his God and followed through by telling the strongest man on the planet what to do.

Lead with Humility

And the thing was good in the eyes of Pharaoh, and in the eyes of all his servants.

Genesis 41:37

This says a lot about Pharaoh. Earlier, we learned that Pharaoh made a feast for all his servants on his own birthday (Gen. 40:20). It may seem like a small thing, but how many leaders make a feast for their servants, to tell them that they are appreciated? I think this is an insight into Pharaoh—that he wasn't as arrogant as what we typically think of other pharaohs, like Rameses, the one who was pharaoh during the time of Moses.

But this pharaoh considered his servants—maybe not perfectly, because he took the baker, cut his head off, and hung him on a tree so the birds could eat him (Gen. 40:22)—but he did make a feast on his birthday for his servants. And later, Pharaoh humbled himself and listened to a prisoner. That sort of thing is uncharacteristic of absolute dictators.

I don't know if this was an exception to the way Pharaoh normally was. Maybe he was so impacted by these dreams and he saw God use Joseph in such a miraculous way that his heart bore witness with it. It could also be an indication that this pharaoh really had some wisdom, and he was operating in some humility.

For Christians, our humility should naturally flow out of a relationship with God. Jesus should not just be your Savior; He should be your Lord. If you have truly bowed the knee—if you're a living sacrifice (Rom. 12:1)—then you are humble. It's an inevitable byproduct of your relationship with Him.

My whole life is built on just doing whatever God tells me to do. To the best of my ability, I am going to follow God. I am not in charge. I just say, "God, what do You want to do? Whatever it is, my answer is yes before You even ask." If God tells you to do something, and you sit there and chafe at it, then you are not humble. You are not trusting God, and you are going to be a poor leader. Even if he didn't believe in the God of Joseph when he had those dreams, Pharaoh at least had the humility to recognize they had significance and needed to be interpreted.

We don't know exactly how long this took, but the scripture says it was good in the eyes of Pharaoh's servants. That means that Pharaoh at least looked to his servants, or maybe he consulted with them, and it was unanimous among all of them. To get a unanimous verdict from people is hard to do. This is an indication that Joseph had just seized the day.

Let God Promote You

It had taken thirteen years, but God had prepared Joseph and put him into position. God opened a door that no man could shut (Rev. 3:8). God will do that. He will promote you. But I think it's significant to recognize that Joseph didn't promote himself. Joseph didn't fight back against his brothers. He didn't fight back against Potiphar when he was falsely accused. He didn't do any of these things. Joseph was just seeking God. He let God promote him.

When God is in charge of your promotion, then you don't have to sit there and worry about it. But when you promote yourself, you're going to have an Ishmael on your hands because you're trying to produce something on your own (Gen. 16:1–16).

I'm telling you, if you will serve God and seek Him with your whole heart, God will make you look good. God will put you in positions and give you authority that, in the natural, you could have never obtained.

Now, I admit there's a huge difference between Joseph and me, but there are also similarities. If I were God, I wouldn't have chosen me. I'm a college dropout. I'm a "hick from Texas." By the world's standards, there are a lot of negatives in my life. And yet, God has promoted me, given me influence, and allowed me to touch other people.

If I sat down and thought about it, I could name hundreds of people alive today who would have been dead if I hadn't shared God's Word with them, prayed with them, and seen them healed. I can show you marriages changed. I can show you people's lives that were changed. There are some similarities with Joseph in the sense that God has blessed me and made me look good.

I once had somebody ask, "How do you do all of this?" And I said, "I don't really have a clue." I've often said it's like being on a roller coaster—I'm just strapped in, holding on for dear life. I am not controlling what's happening. I'm just seeking God, and He has given me the opportunity to influence and touch a lot of people's lives.

God will make you look good if you'll let Him. But the problem is, most people say to God, "I can handle it. You just get me introduced and give me an opportunity, and I can take it from there." That may be the very reason that God hadn't used you yet.

Satan is going to come against you and try to destroy you. And if you don't have the character to be able to handle the promotion God gives you, it will hurt you. One of the reasons God doesn't promote people is because He loves them too much, but He also loves the people who would be underneath them. He doesn't want someone to become a bad example and discourage other people. So, it just takes time for God to work. But if you allow it, God will put you into a position just like Joseph.

Trust God's Plans

And Pharaoh said unto his servants, Can we find such a one as this is, *a man in whom the Spirit of God* is? *And Pharaoh said unto Joseph, Forasmuch as God hath shewed thee all this,* there is *none so discreet and wise as thou* art: *thou shalt be over my house, and according unto thy word shall all my people be ruled: only in the throne will I be greater than thou. And Pharaoh said unto Joseph, See, I have set thee over all the land of Egypt. And Pharaoh took off his ring from his hand, and put it upon Joseph's hand, and arrayed him in vestures of fine linen, and put a gold chain about his neck; and he made him to ride in the second chariot which he had; and they cried before him,*

Bow the knee: and he made him ruler *over all the land of Egypt. And Pharaoh said unto Joseph, I am Pharaoh, and without thee shall no man lift up his hand or foot in all the land of Egypt.*

Genesis 41:38–44

The ring is how Pharaoh would seal things. It was his official mark, like a notary. And once he made things official, he took off that same ring and gave it to Joseph. That is just nearly too good to believe! If this wasn't in the Bible, you would think somebody made it up. How could a person go from the pit to the palace in just an hour's time?

It probably didn't take very long for Pharaoh to tell his dreams and for Joseph to interpret them. Then, Joseph gave him instructions, and Pharaoh was willing to turn over the reins of the entire nation to a man the Egyptians despised and who had just come out of prison. That is miraculous!

God has a plan for your life just as surely as he had a plan for Joseph's life, but you may not see it. Joseph didn't really see evidence of it for thirteen years. Everything looked like it was going against Joseph, but he held onto those dreams that God gave him. And then, he went from the pit to the palace overnight.

Everybody wants success, but very few people are willing to go through what Joseph went through to get there. One of the reasons God gives you visions and dreams is because in between when He shows you His will for your life and when you see it come to pass, there's going to be opposition. If you never run into the devil, it's probably because you're both headed in the same direction.

When you turn around and start going God's way, there's going to be resistance. It takes more effort not to just go with the flow—to go along to get along. But, sad to say, that's what most people are doing. They just want to fritter their time away, keep themselves occupied, and take the path of least resistance.

You are never going to obtain God's best for your life if you just do what's convenient. You need to have a vision from God; you need to hold on to it and stand through the opposition that's going to come your way. Most people aren't willing to do that. Many people want the results Joseph got, but they aren't willing to go through what Joseph went through.

I've had people come to Charis Bible College, and they see that I'm blessed. My house and cars are paid for. I don't owe any money on anything, and people think, *Well, God did that for Andrew, so He'll do it for me.* That's absolutely true, but what you don't realize is that I went through a lot of things to get from where I started to where I am now. I didn't immediately see God's provision. I kept going at times when everybody around me said I should quit. I think the only person who hasn't told me to quit and give up is Jamie. God put Jamie and me together supernaturally, and she's stood with me; but there were times we didn't have another person on this planet who believed the vision God had put in my heart would come to pass.

Everybody wants our results, but not everybody's willing to go through what we went through to get there. I'm not blaming God because a lot of my problems were self-inflicted. I don't think anybody does everything perfectly, but you are going to have to stand. You will make some mistakes along the way, but you've got to keep yourself encouraged.

Encourage Yourself

David was anointed by God when he was about seventeen years old (1 Sam. 16:13), just like Joseph. He was 30 years old when he was anointed to be king (2 Sam. 5:3–4). So, it was the exact same length of time before David saw God's vision begin to come to pass. The night before David became king, it looked like everything had failed. His hometown had been invaded. His family and those of all his men had been taken captive (1 Sam. 30:1–6). His soldiers spoke of stoning him. For thirteen years, he had been faithful, and yet everything looked like it was going against him. But it says in 1 Samuel 30:6, *"David encouraged himself in the LORD his God."*

In a situation where his family was taken captive, his city had been burned, his own men were in revolt, and they were thinking of killing him, David encouraged himself in the Lord.

And within twenty-four hours, he was king (2 Sam. 5:3). His vision came to pass, but he was right up against it and tempted to quit. He cried until he had no more power to weep (1 Sam. 30:4). This was not something that just rolled off his back. It was a severe test, and yet he stood and encouraged himself.

If you've got dreams in your heart and yet it looks like none of them are coming to pass, you may be thinking of quitting. Are you going to give up? Are you going to get bitter at God? David didn't do that. And Joseph didn't do that either.

Joseph was promoted over the entire land of Egypt just hours after sitting in prison. David became the king within just hours of encouraging himself against all odds. Everything worked out for them, and everything's going to work out for you *if* you don't give up. In Galatians 6:9, the apostle Paul wrote, *"in due season we shall reap, if we faint not,"* but that's a big "if." Sad to say, most people faint.

Jeremiah 12:5 says, *"If thou hast run with the footmen, and they have wearied thee, then how canst thou contend with horses?"* In other words, Jeremiah is saying, "If small things have worn you out and you're going to give up, what are you going to do when something really big happens?" If God has destined for you to be in a position of influence and leadership, I guarantee you, the moment you get there, you are going to be attacked. You're going to have people come out against you.

When I was in the army, I got in trouble for not properly saluting my superiors. I don't know what it was about giving a salute, but I just had a hard time doing it. The situation got so serious that I was threatened with discipline—so, I started saluting everything that moved! When I got deployed to Vietnam and sent to a fire support base, I saw a colonel walking toward me one day, so I stopped and saluted. That colonel knocked me down, stood over me, and said, "If you ever see this bald head coming toward you again, you'd better turn and go the other way!"

As I was lying there, I thought, *Which is it? Do I salute or not salute?* But that colonel explained to me that enemy snipers were watching the base, and if they saw someone get saluted, they knew he was an officer. Officers were at higher risk of being shot because they were leaders. If the men lost their leader, they could fall into disarray and give the enemy an advantage in case of attack.

It's the same way in the kingdom of God. If you are serving God, you've got a big target drawn on you, and if you can't handle the situation you're in right now, you'll never be able to handle it when God promotes you. I think that's one of the reasons it took thirteen years for Joseph to be promoted, from the time God gave him these visions until he stood before Pharaoh. It just takes time for God to work that kind of integrity in you. That's really powerful!

Overcome Self-Centeredness

And Pharaoh called Joseph's name Zaphnath-paaneah; and he gave him to wife Asenath the daughter of Potipherah priest of On. And Joseph went out over all the land of Egypt. And Joseph was thirty years old when he stood before Pharaoh king of Egypt. And Joseph went out from the presence of Pharaoh, and went throughout all the land of Egypt.

Genesis 41:45–46

Now compare this with Genesis 37:2, where it says Joseph was seventeen years old when those dreams came to him. He was thirty years old when he stood before Pharaoh. That's thirteen years since God gave him the vision, and for all that time, not a single thing looked good. Joseph was just taking one step down after another.

Joseph went from being loved by his father, to being rejected by his brothers, to being sold into slavery, to being lied about and falsely accused of rape, to being put in prison. Then, the man he helped get out of prison forgot about him for two years. All these things looked like just a cascade of failures, and nothing was working.

Maybe you have had less happen to you than what happened to Joseph, and yet you have convinced yourself that the world is against you—that nothing is working. Joseph had more reasons to complain, become depressed, and to quit than any of us have, and yet he didn't take those opportunities.

These days, it seems like there is more depression than ever. It seems like the number of people who are diagnosed with depression and take medication for it has skyrocketed. But I don't believe it's because people's situations are worse; it's because people are not as strong. People have become *"lovers of their own themselves,"* and *"lovers of pleasures more than lovers of God"* (2 Tim. 3:2–4).

During World War II, there were people who laid down their lives, knowing they were going to die. Jamie's uncle, James, was in the first wave of U.S. Marines who landed on the beaches of Iwo Jima. His superiors told them the first five waves of men, with a thousand men in each wave, would probably not survive. They were just used to draw the fire from the Japanese forces holding the island, and it was likely the first 5,000 Americans would be killed. They had to do that in order to establish a beachhead on Iwo Jima. James contacted his family, knowing that he was probably going to die because he was in the first wave, but he was willing to lay his life down. He had a cause that was bigger than himself.

Sad to say, there are very few people that would be willing to lay down their life today. It may be that one of the reasons God can't promote you is because you couldn't handle it. When you get promoted, you're going to become a target for the enemy. Satan's going to fight against you. If you are not willing to lay down your life for a cause, you won't overcome because you don't have any integrity. I'm not saying that to criticize, but I am saying it to open your eyes. If you want God to use you, become usable. Quit asking God to promote you and thinking about how to advance yourself. Think about how you can serve other people.

Secure God's Provision

And in the seven plenteous years the earth brought forth by handfuls. And he gathered up all the food of the seven years, which were in the land of Egypt, and laid up the food in the cities: the food of the field, which was round about every city, laid he up in the same. And Joseph gathered corn as the sand of the sea, very much, until he left numbering; for it was without number.

Genesis 41:47–49

This is speaking of abundance and was exactly what Joseph said would happen. These were good times for Joseph and all of Egypt. But Joseph's advancement was all because of his prophecy of the seven years of famine. If they had never come, Joseph would have been viewed as a charlatan instead of a hero. He could have faced severe consequences.

One of the greatest testimonies to Joseph's faith in the Lord was during these seven years of plenty. It's one thing to serve the Lord when you're in crisis. When Joseph was sold into slavery and then put in prison, what else could he do? The only other option was to give up and quit. But if he ever wanted to see his dreams come to pass, he had to trust in God.

To Joseph's credit, he was as committed to God during the years of prosperity as he was during the years of trial. A person can be at greater risk of getting in trouble during prosperity than during hardship. Nearly everyone turns to the Lord when they are in trouble, but when everything seems to be good, few stay dependent upon the Lord.

Joseph followed the Lord's leading and stored food in cities, anticipating the day he would distribute it. The food wasn't stored in one place but was scattered among the cities for easy access. This was wisdom and planning in advance. Men often squander God's provision and therefore don't prosper during their time of need.

And unto Joseph were born two sons before the years of famine came, which Asenath the daughter of Poti-pherah priest of On bare unto him. And Joseph called the name of the firstborn Manasseh: For God, said he, hath made me forget all my toil, and all my father's house. And the name of the second called he Ephraim: For God hath caused me to be fruitful in the land of my affliction.

Genesis 41:50–52

Joseph had two sons in the first seven years of his marriage to Asenath. The name *Manasseh* means "causing to forget."[6] I believe this refers to Joseph forgetting all the trouble he endured and the terrible things done to him by his brothers. I don't believe Joseph "forgot" about his family, but he wasn't bitter about what happened. He focused his attention on the goodness God had shown him and was busy doing what the Lord called him to do.

The name *Ephraim* means "double fruit."[7] Joseph was praising God for the abundance and fruitfulness He had provided. This might also have been prophetic since Joseph got twice the inheritance of any of his brothers (Gen. 48:21–22).

And the seven years of plenteousness, that was in the land of Egypt, were ended. And the seven years of dearth began to come, according as Joseph had said: and the dearth was in all lands; but in all the land of Egypt there was bread. And when all the land of Egypt was famished, the people cried to Pharaoh for bread: and Pharaoh said unto all the Egyptians, Go unto Joseph; what he saith to you, do. And the famine was over all the face of the earth: and Joseph opened all the storehouses, and sold unto the Egyptians; and the famine waxed sore in the land of Egypt. And all countries came into Egypt to Joseph for to buy corn; because that the famine was so sore in all lands.

Genesis 41:53–57

This is amazing! Joseph had stored up so much food, he was selling to the people what had once been theirs. This provided a windfall for the Egyptian government. He also supplied food not only to the Egyptians but also to the other countries around Egypt. In the midst of all this, Pharaoh was exercising uncommon wisdom for a government leader. Most people would have taken credit for seeing the famine coming, and their arrogance would have caused them to take over when it was convenient, but Pharoah continued directing people to Joseph. Pharaoh showed remarkable humility and wisdom in this.

Joseph's faithfulness to God affected not only all of Egypt but also many surrounding countries. It's true God prepared everything to protect His children, so the Israelites could come to Egypt and be supernaturally sustained by Joseph, but He was not only concerned about His people. God showed these things to Pharaoh, to prepare him, bless all of the Egyptians, and keep them and other nations from starving. The goodness of God is not only shown in the fact that He gave Pharaoh dreams telling him what was to come. But the Lord also sent seven years of plenty before He sent seven years of famine. There is always provision before there is need.

Chapter 10

Vengeance Is the Lord's

Now when Jacob saw that there was corn in Egypt, Jacob said unto his sons, Why do ye look one upon another? And he said, Behold, I have heard that there is corn in Egypt: get you down thither, and buy for us from thence; that we may live, and not die. And Joseph's ten brethren went down to buy corn in Egypt. But Benjamin, Joseph's brother, Jacob sent not with his brethren; for he said, Lest peradventure mischief befall him.

Genesis 42:1–4

Abraham and Isaac both endured famines in their lifetimes (Gen. 12:10 and 26:1–3). Abraham went into Egypt to survive, but Isaac stayed in the land, sowed, and reaped a hundredfold return in his year of famine (Gen. 26:12). Here, Jacob and his family experienced another famine.

If Jacob had tried to do what his father, Isaac, did during the famine in his days, it wouldn't have worked. Isaac had a word from God to stay in the land and the Lord would bless him (Gen. 26:2–4). Jacob didn't have that word. It was just natural for Jacob to go where the food was. The Lord used this to establish His plans for the nation of Israel.

There is always a balance between doing what is natural and following the Lord. It all boils down to what the Lord is saying. If we have a word from the Lord, we follow it regardless of carnal wisdom. If we don't have a word from the Lord, we need to take practical steps to meet our needs.

This goes to show that bad things can happen to those who are blessed, but it also shows that God provides for His people even during hard times. God had given dreams to Pharaoh before the famine came. He always provides the supply before we have the need. Nothing takes God by surprise.

The drought became severe in the land of Canaan, so Jacob told ten of his sons to go to Egypt to buy food. In his mind, Joseph had already died and Benjamin, Jacob's youngest son, was the only other son that was born through his favorite wife Rachel (Gen. 35:24). Jacob loved Rachel the most (Gen. 29:30). Since he thought Joseph was dead, Jacob hung on to Benjamin and wouldn't let him leave home.

Joseph's brothers had no idea what was about to happen to them. But the Lord had planned this for more than twenty years. It would change all their lives as well as the history of Israel. They were about to play a role in fulfilling the vision God gave Joseph all those years before.

As a slave and a prisoner, Joseph couldn't do anything to bring God's vision to pass. But when he became the most powerful man in Egypt outside of Pharaoh, he had access to armies and every other resource. Joseph could have gone back to his family, taken an army with him and he could have forced his brothers to bow before him. But he didn't do that. Joseph waited another nine years after he had absolute authority; he waited on God to bring those visions to pass. To me, that is the greatest indication of the true heart and character of Joseph.

Avoid Being a Self-Promoter

Pride is defined in a lot of different ways. Most people think pride is simply arrogance, such as when you think you're better than everybody else. However, low self-esteem should also be considered prideful even though most people think low self-esteem is humility.

I believe that one of the core values of humility is not being self-willed and self-dependent. There are so many scriptures that go along with this.

> *Trust in the LORD with all thine heart; and lean not unto thine own understanding. In all thy ways acknowledge him, and he shall direct thy paths.*
>
> Proverbs 3:5–6

For promotion cometh *neither from the east, nor from the west, nor from the south. But God* is *the judge: he putteth down one, and setteth up another.*

Psalm 75:6–7

One of the distinguishing characteristics of true godly humility is not promoting yourself. Now, that doesn't mean you won't be promoted. But instead of exalting yourself, you commit yourself to God and let Him be the one who promotes you.

1 Peter 5:6 says,

Humble yourselves therefore under the mighty hand of God, that he may exalt you in due time.

A humble person is not a self-promoter, not self-willed, and doesn't try to make things come to pass. This virtue is missing in the vast majority of people today. The moment they have the power to make those visions come to pass on their own, they do it. But Joseph remained faithful and waited on God to bring things to pass. He humbled himself, and God exalted him in due season. He never forgot his dreams (Gen. 37:7, 9).

It's one thing to not gripe and complain when there's nothing you can do, but after Joseph became the lord over the whole land, he could have made those dreams come to pass. If he was just bitter, wanting to get back at his brothers and punish them, he could have done it. But for nine years, Joseph just did what God had anointed him to do. He didn't do one thing to make his dreams come to pass.

In Psalm 105:19, the Scripture says of Joseph, *"until the time that his word came: the word of the LORD tried him."* The Word was what dominated Joseph and kept him going throughout the entire time, and when he had the ability to bring it to pass in his own strength, he didn't do it. Joseph was a God-dependent man. He was totally trusting in God, and the reason he was promoted is because he wasn't self-willed.

We need to let God be the one who defends and promotes us, but most people only turn to God to get over a crisis. And the moment it looks like the crisis is over, they will go back to doing things their own way—what got them into the crisis in the first place! That may be the very reason those people haven't seen God's will come to pass in their lives.

Fulfill the Dream

And the sons of Israel came to buy corn *among those that came: for the famine was in the land of Canaan. And Joseph* was *the governor over the land,* and *he* it was *that sold to all the people of the land: and Joseph's brethren came, and bowed down themselves before him* with *their faces to the earth.*

Genesis 42:5–6

This was consistent with the vision Joseph had seen (Gen. 37:7), but it wasn't the completion of the vision. It wasn't just about his brothers bowing down to him. They came and bowed down more times than that (Gen. 43:26, 28, and 44:14). I believe Joseph knew that his dreams (Gen. 37:5–11) would be fulfilled through his position in Egypt. That's why he was the one selling the corn instead of delegating that to a subordinate. He was looking forward to this day.

Remember that Joseph had two dreams. The first one showed all eleven of his brothers bowing down to him (Gen. 37:5–7), but only ten of his brothers were present in this instance. I'm sure none of Joseph's brothers expected to ever see Joseph again, much less bow to him, but they may have thought of him and wondered what became of him. This was going to be the biggest shock of their lives!

> *And Joseph saw his brethren, and he knew them, but made himself strange unto them, and spake roughly unto them; and he said unto them, Whence come ye? And they said, From the land of Canaan to buy food. And Joseph knew his brethren, but they knew not him. And Joseph remembered the dreams which he dreamed of them, and said unto them, Ye are spies; to see the nakedness of the land ye are come.*
>
> Genesis 42:7–9

Joseph was only seventeen years old when (Gen. 37:27–28) his brothers sold him into slavery, so he had changed a lot. Plus, he had on all the Egyptian garb. Every time you see pictures of the rulers in ancient Egypt, they had on headdresses and other things. So, while Joseph may have looked different to them, he was able to easily recognize his brethren.

I believe most people think the way Joseph treated his brothers was out of bitterness and revenge. He was trying to hurt them as much as they had hurt him. And that's the way that I've heard nearly all other teachers present this. But I do not believe that's the case at all. People who harbor unforgiveness and bitterness don't behave themselves with the kind of integrity Joseph exhibited throughout his entire life.

Joseph's brothers were evil, ungodly men. Back in those days, they didn't have the government control that we see today. The Bible says there was a time when there was no king in Israel, and every man did that which was right in his own eyes (Judges 17:6 and 21:25). When the brothers came down to Egypt, they found a government there, but in the land of Canaan, there wasn't a king. People did pretty much what they wanted to, and they did some pretty bad things.

Remember that Reuben, the oldest son of Jacob, committed incest with one of his father's wives (Gen. 32:28 and 35:10). Simeon and Levi murdered hundreds of men in Shechem and took all of the women and the children captive. Judah committed incest with his own daughter-in-law, and she got pregnant and had twins by him (Gen. 38:12–27). Even Issachar and Zebulun were consenting to the treatment of Joseph (Gen. 37:18–20). These were some bad dudes. They were lawless and doing whatever they wanted. God not only preserved their life by sending Joseph ahead of them into Egypt to prepare for a famine, but part of the vision He gave to Joseph was to see these brothers finally bow their knee to God.

I believe Joseph recognized God was trying to bring these men to the end of themselves. They were going to be the leaders of the twelve tribes of Israel. That would be their legacy. But these guys were bad, and God was trying to bring them back to a place to where they recognized His authority. They had to humble themselves.

The reason Joseph accused his brothers of being spies wasn't because he was bitter, and he was not trying to punish them. He saw God put him into this position. He saw that these men needed to humble and come to the end of themselves.

Refuse to Compromise

And they said unto him, Nay, my lord, but to buy food are thy servants come. We are *all one man's sons; we* are *true* men, *thy servants are no spies. And he said unto them, Nay, but to see the nakedness of the land ye are come. And they said, Thy servants* are *twelve brethren, the sons of one man in the land of Canaan; and, behold, the youngest is* this day *with our father, and one* is *not.*

Genesis 42:10–13

Of course, Joseph knew all of this. They were saying that one brother died, but he hadn't really died. They were speaking about Joseph. He was the ruler who was accusing them of being spies, but they didn't know it. Now, they may not have been spies, but it was stretching the truth to say they were all true men. As it turns out, these brothers ended up calling the one whom they once despised "lord." God's justice is awesome!

And Joseph said unto them, That is it *that I spake unto you, saying, Ye* are *spies: hereby ye shall be proved: By the life of Pharaoh ye shall not go forth hence, except your youngest brother come hither. Send one of you, and let him fetch your brother, and ye shall be kept in prison, that your words may be proved, whether* there be any *truth in you: or else by the life of Pharaoh surely ye* are *spies.*

Genesis 42:14–16

What would have happened if Joseph had revealed himself to his brothers right here? There is no way to know for sure, but I know that wasn't what God had planned. Joseph's dream clearly showed eleven brothers bowing down to him (Gen. 37:9). Regardless of how much Joseph wanted to reveal

141

himself, he needed to stick to God's plan. The Lord was going to use Joseph to bring his brothers to the end of themselves.

Likewise, we need to stay the course when pursuing God's will. There will always be opportunities to compromise and do things some easier way. Compromise is the language of the devil. Satan offered Jesus an easier way to obtain His goal (Matt. 4:8–9 and Luke 4:5–7). But praise God, He didn't take it!

In this case, Joseph wasn't about to compromise. He was making them prove their testimony by bringing Benjamin back to him. This would prolong the pressure on them and guarantee he would see his younger brother. The Lord clearly showed Joseph that all eleven of his brothers would bow to him (Gen. 37:5–11). This necessitated Benjamin coming with them.

Reap What Is Sown

And he put them all together into ward three days. And Joseph said unto them the third day, This do, and live; for *I fear God: if ye* be *true* men, *let one of your brethren be bound in the house of your prison: go ye, carry corn for the famine of your houses: but bring your youngest brother unto me; so shall your words be verified, and ye shall not die. And they did so. And they said one to another, We* are *verily guilty concerning our brother, in that we saw the*

anguish of his soul, when he besought us, and we would
not hear; therefore is this distress come upon us.

Genesis 42:17–21

These brothers had never lost the guilt of what they had done to Joseph. Contrary to the old saying, it's deception to think that "time heals all wounds." Only God and forgiveness do that. Even though the account in Genesis 37 doesn't tell us, it's from this passage that we learn Joseph pleaded with his brothers for his life when he was thrown in the pit. Over the years, they must have replayed those thoughts in their minds over and over again. It's no wonder, then, that the brothers realized they were reaping what they had sown (Gal. 6:7).

This is also a picture of what hell must be like. Along with constant pain, thirst, and suffering, those in hell will have to deal with all their regrets and memories of past sins. Jesus taught that hell is a place of torment, and memory will be part of that torment:

But Abraham said, Son, remember that thou in thy
lifetime receivedst thy good things, and likewise Lazarus
evil things: but now he is comforted, and thou art
tormented.

Luke 16:25

In contrast, the Bible tells us heaven is a place where Jesus will wipe all tears away from our eyes, and there will be no more death, sorrow, crying, or pain (Rev. 7:17 and 21:4). The Lord spoke through Isaiah about the righteous in the future creation, and how there will be no regret, guilt, or shame:

For, behold, I create new heavens and a new earth: and the former shall not be remembered, nor come into mind.

Isaiah 65:17

Heaven will be so glorious that, unlike the rich man in hell (Luke 16:19–31), all the sufferings of this life will never come to mind for those who are forever united with the Lord in heaven. That's awesome!

Now, unlike hell, which will be cast into the lake of fire for eternity along with every person in it, Joseph's brothers were only kept in prison for three days. To be fair, Joseph spent years in slavery and in prison because of their actions. Joseph could have easily and justifiably locked them up and thrown away the key, but he had pity on them—not only them, but also on his father and all the family members who were back in Canaan. Joseph knew that keeping his brothers in prison for an extended period would put a hardship on all their families and his father.

I'm sure there were other ways that the brothers' story could have been vetted. But Joseph never really thought they were spies. This was just his way of getting them to bring Benjamin to him. Benjamin was the only brother who had not hated Joseph, and he was Joseph's only full-blood brother (Gen. 43:30).

Be Bitter or Better

And Reuben answered them, saying, Spake I not unto you, saying, Do not sin against the child; and ye would not hear? therefore, behold, also his blood is required. And they knew not that Joseph understood them; for he spake unto them by an interpreter. And he turned himself about from them, and wept; and returned to them again, and communed with them, and took from them Simeon, and bound him before their eyes.

Genesis 42:22–24

After twenty-two years in Egypt, Joseph had clearly mastered the Egyptian language. He likely didn't speak with an accent of any kind. Also, he spoke through an interpreter. His brothers had no way of suspecting Joseph spoke their language, so they spoke freely in front of him. They also weren't around any of their fellow countrymen, so they assumed none of what they said would get back to their father in Canaan. They held nothing back, which revealed to Joseph what would otherwise be part of private conversations.

Reuben didn't participate with his brothers in their plot to kill Joseph; he planned to set Joseph free and return him to his father (Gen. 37:21–22). But Reuben did participate with his brothers in lying to Jacob about Joseph's death. Therefore, he was just as guilty as they were.

Joseph never knew Reuben pleaded with the others to save his life. This was new information for him and probably had a profound impact. It may have caused Joseph to select another brother and let Reuben depart. Simeon, one of the cruelest of Joseph's brothers (Gen. 34:25), became a hostage until Benjamin came.

Even though what Reuben said caused Joseph to weep, he kept his composure in front of his brothers. He couldn't let his emotions get in the way of what God was trying to do through him. All of us have had negative experiences. The choice is ours whether we become bitter or better as a result. If anyone could have been bitter, it was Joseph. But God had given him a vision and he held on to that, even when he could have broken down and just revealed himself to his brothers before the right time. Joseph remained faithful.

Then Joseph commanded to fill their sacks with corn, and to restore every man's money into his sack, and to give them provision for the way: and thus did he unto them. And they laded their asses with the corn, and departed thence. And as one of them opened his sack to give his ass provender in the inn, he espied his money; for, behold, it was in his sack's mouth. And he said unto his brethren,

My money is restored; and, lo, it is even in my sack: and
their heart failed them, and they were afraid, saying one
to another, What is this that God hath done unto us?

Genesis 42:25–28

Simeon, the second-oldest son of Jacob, was put in prison, and the other nine brothers went back home. As they went home, they stopped along the way at one of the inns and opened up their sacks to be able to get something to feed their animals. When they opened their sacks, they found all the money they had brought to purchase grain. They said, *"What is this that God hath done unto us?"* (Gen. 42:28). They'd been accused of being spies, and now they had all their money back. They were afraid they were going to be accused of stealing the money that belonged to Pharaoh. It says, *"their heart failed them, and they were afraid"* (Gen. 42:28).

Again, we get to choose whether to be bitter or better. In this case, Joseph was showing favor to his brethren, not hatred. His actions were to facilitate God breaking their stubborn pride. What must have been going through their minds and hearts? Based on what they spoke of in front of Joseph, they must have felt like their sins had come home to roost (Num. 32:23).

The brothers were beginning to recognize God's hand in all of this. They didn't know the end result of all this would be a blessing because, at this time, they were fearful that doom awaited them. The Lord orchestrated everything in a way that would never be forgotten by them. Joseph could have revealed himself to his brothers and made his dreams come to pass on his own, but that wouldn't have been part of God's plan. That wouldn't have broken them and brought them to the end of themselves.

Show Mercy

And they came unto Jacob their father unto the land of Canaan, and told him all that befell unto them; saying, The man, who is the lord of the land, spake roughly to us, and took us for spies of the country. And we said unto him, We are true men; we are no spies: we be twelve brethren, sons of our father; one is not, and the youngest is this day with our father in the land of Canaan.

Genesis 42:29–32

They went back home, and they met with Jacob, their father. And they had to tell him why Simeon wasn't with them. He was being held in prison. If they had told Jacob all the truth twenty-two years before when they led him to believe Joseph had been killed, they wouldn't have been in this situation. At this point, they were still putting forth the lie about Joseph being dead. They had not repented from their ungodly ways and wouldn't take any responsibility for their actions.

The very fact that Joseph allowed them to take the food for their families should have tipped them off that he wasn't as bad as they might have perceived him to be. He was being very merciful toward people who thought they were accused as spies. There were signs of God's goodness, but their guilty consciences only allowed them to see the negative.

> *And the man, the lord of the country, said unto us, Hereby shall I know that ye are true men; leave one of your brethren here with me, and take food for the famine of your households, and be gone: And bring your youngest brother unto me: then shall I know that ye are no spies, but that ye are true men: so will I deliver you your brother, and ye shall traffick in the land. And it came to pass as they emptied their sacks, that, behold, every man's bundle of money was in his sack: and when both they and their father saw the bundles of money, they were afraid.*
>
> Genesis 42:33–35

The brothers told Jacob they couldn't go back and get any more food unless they brought along Benjamin. Again, the dream God gave Joseph when he was seventeen years old showed all eleven of his brothers bowing down to him, so Benjamin had to come to Egypt to bring it to fulfillment.

Also, all their money being returned to them should not have been seen as an accident. Finding one person's money might have been explained away. But to have everyone's money in their sacks was no accident. This was obviously done intentionally, but for what purpose?

I suspect Joseph had this all planned in advance. His dreams prepared him for the day when his brothers would come and bow down to him. It was only logical to think that his brothers would have to come to Egypt for food during the famine. Joseph probably prayed about this and was inspired by the Lord in his actions.

The Root of All Grief

And Jacob their father said unto them, Me have ye bereaved of my children: Joseph is not, and Simeon is not, and ye will take Benjamin away: all these things are against me. And Reuben spake unto his father, saying, Slay my two sons, if I bring him not to thee: deliver him into my hand, and I will bring him to thee again. And he said, My son shall not go down with you; for his brother is dead, and he is left alone: if mischief befall him by the way in the which ye go, then shall ye bring down my gray hairs with sorrow to the grave.

Genesis 42:36–38

Jacob was willing to count Simeon as dead in order to save Benjamin. He was thinking about the worst-case scenario: if

Benjamin went to Egypt and didn't come back, then he would lose Joseph, Simeon, and Benjamin. At this point, Jacob was willing to cut his losses and just keep Benjamin. Remember, Jacob was still grieving for Joseph and refused to be comforted (Gen. 37:34–35). He was willing to let another son sit in prison for an indefinite amount of time rather than part with the youngest son of his favorite wife. Jacob was being selfish. That's just terrible.

Grief is rooted in self-centeredness. When a loved one dies, we tearfully ask ourselves, "How can I go on without them?" Giving in to strong emotions, we focus on the death and loss, crying, "I won't ever see them alive on earth again!" Then we convince ourselves our mourning is for the dead, when it's really for ourselves.

If the deceased person you're grieving over was saved and now in heaven, there is much to celebrate. Your loved one now stands in the presence of Jesus, receiving their eternal reward! Can you imagine the atmosphere of a believer's funeral if you weren't so self-centered? Instead of crisis, what an exciting time of thanksgiving, praise, and rejoicing it would be!

Truly, grief comes because of selfishness. Pain and loss may seem more real to you than the truth of your loved one's happiness and peace in heaven, but stop and ask yourself, "Why am I really grieving? Is this sorrow for them or for me?" An honest answer will reveal the selfishness in your heart.

Chapter 11

Come to the End of Yourself

And the famine was sore in the land. And it came to pass, when they had eaten up the corn which they had brought out of Egypt, their father said unto them, Go again, buy us a little food. And Judah spake unto him, saying, The man did solemnly protest unto us, saying, Ye shall not see my face, except your brother be with you. If thou wilt send our brother with us, we will go down and buy thee food: But if thou wilt not send him, we will not go down: for the man said unto us, Ye shall not see my face, except your brother be with you.

Genesis 43:1–5

When the grain began to run out and they needed more food, Jacob told the brothers to go back to Egypt and buy some more. And they said, "If we go back, we are going to be considered spies. The only way we'll go back is if you let us bring Benjamin."

Joseph had made it clear for them not to come back unless Benjamin was with them. They feared what would happen if they went without him. Joseph didn't specify what the conse-quences would be, but it was certain they would be taken as spies. That could have meant death or certainly imprisonment.

Now, think about Simeon. These scriptures don't give an exact time between the brothers' first and second visits to Egypt. I would think the food they purchased lasted some time, so Simeon had been in prison for months at the very least. Simeon knew how long it took to travel from Canaan to Egypt, and that his brothers would have already returned if Jacob had given them leave.

Simeon must have figured his father abandoned him in favor of keeping Benjamin. I imagine he also had plenty of time to think about his life and what he and his brothers had done to Joseph.

> *And Israel said, Wherefore dealt ye* so *ill with me,* as *to tell the man whether ye had yet a brother? And they said, The man asked us straitly of our state, and of our kindred, saying, Is your father yet alive? have ye* another *brother? and we told him according to the tenor of these words: could we certainly know that he would say, Bring your brother down?*
>
> Genesis 43:6–7

Jacob got mad at his sons and said, *"Wherefore dealt ye so ill with me, as to tell the man whether ye had yet a brother?"* They said, "Well, we didn't know what he was going to do. He just asked us plainly. He asked us about you. He asked if we had any other brothers. And we didn't know what he was going to do, so we just told him the truth." Jacob was only speaking out of his emotions because there was no reason to fault his sons for telling Joseph the truth.

All the same, Jacob was not about to let Benjamin go back with them because he was the remaining son of his favorite wife Rachel (Gen. 42:36–38). He protested loudly (Gen. 43:6), but there was really no choice. Necessity ultimately moved Jacob to do what he said he wouldn't do. They were starving.

> *And Judah said unto Israel his father, Send the lad with me, and we will arise and go; that we may live, and not die, both we, and thou, and also our little ones. I will be surety for him; of my hand shalt thou require him: if I bring him not unto thee, and set him before thee, then let me bear the blame for ever: For except we had lingered, surely now we had returned this second time.*
>
> Genesis 43:8–10

Earlier, Reuben told Jacob he could kill his two sons in Benjamin's place if they didn't bring him back (Gen. 42:37). It was a stupid thing to say, but it did reveal his commitment to bringing Benjamin back alive. Now, Judah said he would be accountable if he didn't bring Benjamin back (Gen. 43:8–10).

Just as with Reuben's rash vow, this wasn't smart. You cannot guarantee things will always work out because some things are beyond your control. But Reuben and Judah showed they were beginning to come to the end of themselves. They were making all kinds of promises to their father because they were in a life-and-death situation. Without more food, they would certainly perish.

> *And their father Israel said unto them, If* it must *be so now, do this; take of the best fruits in the land in your vessels, and carry down the man a present, a little balm, and a little honey, spices, and myrrh, nuts, and almonds: And take double money in your hand; and the money that was brought again in the mouth of your sacks, carry* it *again in your hand; peradventure it* was *an oversight: Take also your brother, and arise, go again unto the man: And God Almighty give you mercy before the man, that he may send away your other brother, and Benjamin. If I be bereaved* of my children, *I am bereaved.*
>
> Genesis 43:11–14

Jacob gave in. He told his sons they could go back, take the money, a lot of gifts, and Benjamin. Jacob told the brothers to take fruit, dates, and all kinds of produce from the land of Canaan to give as a gift to Joseph. Jacob had appeased Esau's anger decades before by gifts (Gen. 32:13–16), and he hoped to do the same in this case (Prov. 18:16).

Israel instructed them to take twice as much money as the first time, plus the money they had found in their sacks. This extra money might have been for restitution or to buy more grain than the first time. Everyone was at a loss as to why their money was in their sacks. None of them could have guessed what really happened.

Then, Jacob said, *"If I be bereaved of* my children, *I am bereaved."* Finally, Jacob just had to come to a place where he was forced into letting Benjamin go with his brothers to Egypt. He pleaded with God for mercy and placed the whole situation in God's hands, which would have been a wise thing to do in the first place.

Fear and Trembling

And the men took that present, and they took double money in their hand, and Benjamin; and rose up, and went down to Egypt, and stood before Joseph. And when Joseph saw Benjamin with them, he said to the ruler of his house, Bring these men home, and slay, and make ready; for these men shall dine with me at noon.

Genesis 43:15–16

They loaded all their animals, took Benjamin, and went back to the land of Egypt to buy more grain. Jacob had smothered Benjamin, as can be seen in the fact that he wouldn't let him go with his brothers to Egypt in the first place. I suspect Benjamin was very excited to finally get free and go to the capital of the mightiest nation on the face of the earth at that time.

When they arrived, Joseph again was the one who was taking the money and seeing who came to buy grain. Of course, Benjamin was much younger than Joseph. Joseph was seventeen years old when he was sold into slavery, so it's very possible he wouldn't have recognized Benjamin right away because he was just a young boy at the time.

Joseph said to the ruler of his house, "Bring them to my house today. I'm going to make a feast for them." I'm sure there was trepidation among the brothers, even though they had complied with Joseph's demands. Instead of feeling honored by the invitation to a personal feast in the house of this virtual ruler of Egypt, they were afraid.

And the man did as Joseph bade; and the man brought the men into Joseph's house. And the men were afraid, because they were brought into Joseph's house; and they said, Because of the money that was returned in our sacks at the first time are we brought in; that he may seek occasion against us, and fall upon us, and take us for bondmen, and our asses.

Genesis 43:17–18

Joseph, being the second-most powerful man in the world, probably had quite a palace. When the brothers were summoned and went to Joseph's house, it says that they trembled and feared what was going to happen because they remembered finding the money in their sacks. I believe Joseph was actually doing this for their good. He was doing it to break them and get them out of their self-will, where they were in defiance of God. Joseph knew that God was using him to bring his brothers to a place of repentance.

I would say one of the biggest misconceptions about Joseph and the way he treated his brothers, is that people think Joseph did these things out of bitterness and unforgiveness. They think he was trying to hurt his brothers as much as they had hurt him. I disagree with that 100 percent.

Now, Joseph might've gotten some satisfaction out of seeing them so vulnerable, but I don't believe that was the motivation for what he was doing. The life of Joseph is not consistent with a person who had been harboring unforgiveness and bitterness. I could take you to many New Testament scriptures (Matt. 6:12–15, 18:21–35; and Col. 3:13) that talk about unforgiveness. A person has got to be able to forgive others. Unforgiveness toward somebody is like drinking poison and hoping the other person will get sick. Actually, unforgiveness will end up killing you.

If Joseph had unforgiveness and bitterness toward his brothers for twenty-two years, I guarantee you, he would not have been flowing in the power and anointing of God the way he was. He would not have been promoted.

Genesis 42:9 says Joseph remembered his dreams, and that's the reason he said, "You are spies." It wasn't because he remembered their treatment of him. It was his dreams (Gen. 37:7, 9). I believe Joseph was doing these things because he knew God had prepared him to preserve their lives through stockpiling food and to bring his brothers to a place of humility before God.

Coming to Repentance

And they came near to the steward of Joseph's house, and they communed with him at the door of the house, And said, O sir, we came indeed down at the first time to buy food: And it came to pass, when we came to the inn, that we opened our sacks, and, behold, every *man's money* was *in the mouth of his sack, our money in full weight: and we have brought it again in our hand. And other money have we brought down in our hands to buy food: we cannot tell who put our money in our sacks.*

Genesis 43:19–22

The brothers were coming clean. They finally humbled themselves. They were telling the truth, hoping that maybe they would avoid being accused of thievery. Most people would have never revealed what happened. They'd hope that no one would know about it, and things would just blow over. But Joseph's brothers believed God was bringing their sins to light (Gen. 42:21–22), and they tried to lessen the impact by coming clean.

> *And he said, Peace be to you, fear not: your God, and the God of your father, hath given you treasure in your sacks: I had your money. And he brought Simeon out unto them. And the man brought the men into Joseph's house, and gave them water, and they washed their feet; and he gave their asses provender.*
>
> Genesis 43:23–24

The wording used here is a specific reference to the God of Abraham, Isaac, and Jacob. This shows the influence of Joseph on those who served him. Joseph had made a spiritual impact on those he came in contact with.

The steward of Joseph's house reassured them and brought Simeon out to them. Simeon had been taken captive the last time they came to Egypt and was in prison since then. So, all of the brothers were finally reunited.

There is no telling what the brothers were thinking. Jacob had said maybe it was an oversight that the money ended up in their sacks; that it was just some kind of a mistake. But now, they knew it wasn't a mistake and that the steward of Joseph's house had put their money back in their sacks. I can just imagine what must've been going through their minds. Joseph had singled them out, accused them of being spies, put their money back in their sacks, and now they were brought to his house for a feast.

Showing Compassion

And they made ready the present against Joseph came at noon: for they heard that they should eat bread there. And when Joseph came home, they brought him the present which was *in their hand into the house, and bowed themselves to him to the earth. And he asked them of* their *welfare, and said,* Is *your father well, the old man of whom ye spake? Is he yet alive? And they answered, Thy servant our father* is *in good health, he* is *yet alive. And they bowed down their heads, and made obeisance.*

Genesis 43:25–28

These are the second and third times the brothers bowed to the earth, but it was the first time all eleven did so. Of course, Joseph was asking about his own father, but they didn't realize that. I'm sure Joseph had been anxious to hear how his father was doing since his first encounter with his brothers.

In the natural, Jacob was old, and there wasn't any guarantee he would still be alive, but Joseph had a dream where his father would come and bow down to him (Gen. 37:9–10). Joseph was acting on God's word to him. As a matter of fact, Jacob was 130 years old when he eventually came into Egypt; he was in good health and lived another seventeen years. In all, he lived to be 147 years old (Gen. 47:28). That's awesome!

And he lifted up his eyes, and saw his brother Benjamin, his mother's son, and said, Is this your younger brother, of whom ye spake unto me? And he said, God be gracious unto thee, my son. And Joseph made haste; for his bowels did yearn upon his brother: and he sought where to weep; and he entered into his chamber, and wept there.

Genesis 43:29–30

The word *bowels* in the Old Testament is used the way we use the word *heart* to describe the seat of our emotions. This shows the love and compassion Joseph had toward his younger brother. He didn't express anger or bitterness in that moment toward his other brothers. Joseph was a man of great character who operated in a tremendous amount of integrity.

It had been twenty-two years since Joseph had been sold into slavery by his brothers. All these men were Joseph's half-brothers, but Benjamin was Joseph's full brother and the only brother who did not participate in selling him into slavery. Benjamin was very young at that time, and he had probably changed a lot. Joseph was still emotional about everything that had happened. He had kept a sensitive heart. I'm sure

Joseph had longed for Benjamin and his father constantly for all those years.

Earning Respect

And he washed his face, and went out, and refrained himself, and said, Set on bread. And they set on for him by himself, and for them by themselves, and for the Egyptians, which did eat with him, by themselves: because the Egyptians might not eat bread with the Hebrews; for that is an abomination unto the Egyptians.

Genesis 43:31–32

This shows the Egyptians thought it was an abomination to even eat with a person who was a Hebrew—and Joseph, even though he was the second-most powerful man in Egypt, was a Hebrew. It shows there was a lot of prejudice among the people during the time. But it does say volumes about Pharaoh; about how he would take a person who was despised for his ethnicity and put him in the second-highest position in the land.

I believe it also says something about Joseph. Even though he had to eat separately, he didn't make a big deal out of it. There are all kinds of prejudices in our world today. And the way the average person deals with it is to say they are owed respect. I believe it's just the opposite. Instead of complaining, griping, and being bitter about it, what you need to do is just earn respect.

Joseph had been so faithful. He interpreted Pharaoh's dreams (Gen. 41:25–32). He had been put in this position where he was over all the Egyptians. He was their master. He could've put them to death, and yet he allowed them to eat separately from him. He didn't force them to respect him. Joseph just did what God gave him opportunity to do, and he earned respect.

I know a Black man who reached the top of his professional sport as a coach. He remembered when he was a child, that his father would not complain about the racial prejudice that was against them. This man's father lived near Washington, DC, for a time, and was not allowed to ride in a bus unless he sat in the back. That was because there were laws that segregated people by skin color. So, rather than suffer that shame and rejection, this man's father just chose to walk everywhere he went. He told his son to not complain, find ways to make things better, and earn people's respect.

Years later, this coach's team finally won a championship and were invited to visit the White House. It was quite an honor. As the team rode a bus through the neighborhoods where his father once walked to work, this coach and his father sat in the very front seat on his way to meet the president of the United States. That's awesome!

That didn't happen because this man complained and demanded respect. He submitted himself to God, embraced opportunities to serve, overcame adversity and disappointment, and worked his way through the ranks to become a successful coach. When he finally achieved success, it was because he had an excellent spirit. In his own words, he found ways to make things better.

There are many other people who would have a chip on their shoulder—who would fight, gripe, and complain. You are not going to be promoted the way Joseph was if that's your attitude. Joseph was over these Egyptians, and yet they wouldn't eat with him because it was a social taboo. He didn't gripe or complain about it. He just dealt with the situation and went on, and God promoted him. That's a great lesson to learn from Joseph.

When I was in the Army, because I witnessed to people and took a stand for the Lord, they called me "Preacher." When I would go into a mess hall and sit down at a table, people would pick up their trays and leave me by myself. I actually went about six to eight weeks without one single person talking to me. They hated me because I had taken a stand and they rejected me.

At one point, there was a race riot when I was in basic training. There were a lot of terrible things happening in the late 1960s, and it was common for violence to break out along racial lines. People became bitter about how they perceived they were being treated and got stirred up. In our barracks, the Black men outnumbered the White men more than to two to one. They blocked the doors, took every White man in the barracks, and beat their heads on the concrete floor. It was terrible.

I was the only White person in that entire barracks who didn't get sent to the infirmary. It was because I had been witnessing to the guy who was beating up everybody. He was a pimp before he joined the military and was just a vicious guy. But I had learned that his father was a Baptist preacher.

This guy knew what he was doing wasn't right. Even though he was drunk and sent thirty or forty White guys to the infirmary, when he came over to my bunk, he stopped. This man picked me up and was probably going to beat me to a pulp just like everybody else. But when he looked at me, I believe God reminded him that I had witnessed to him. So, he just threw me back on my bunk.

I've been hated, but I'm not bitter and angry about it. That's a lesson I learned from Joseph. Hebrews were considered an abomination to the Egyptians, and yet he was second in command over all of Egypt because of his attitude. He didn't let hatred and bitterness get on the inside of him, and he didn't make an issue out of it.

They Marveled at One Another

And they sat before him, the firstborn according to his birthright, and the youngest according to his youth: and the men marvelled one at another. And he took and sent messes unto them from before him: but Benjamin's mess was five times so much as any of theirs. And they drank, and were merry with him.

Genesis 43:33–34

When Joseph's brothers came into his house, they were seated according to their birthright. Now, a lot of people will just skip over this and miss it. But here are these eleven brothers, brought to Joseph's house, and he seated them according to first born, second born, third born, all the way to the youngest—and they marveled at it. They were probably thinking, *How could this Egyptian know this?* Joseph recognized exactly who his brothers were, along with their birth order.

They were not only seated according to their birth order, but then Benjamin was preferred above all the others. Five times as much food was sent to him. That's because Benjamin was the flesh and blood of Joseph, from the same father and mother (Gen. 35:24). These other brothers were half-brothers from different mothers.

The way Joseph seated these brothers according to their birth order and preferred Benjamin just grabbed their attention.

They were looking at each other and wondering, *What is going on?* They knew that something was not normal. They didn't know exactly what was happening, but they knew that it had to be supernatural.

> *And he commanded the steward of his house, saying, Fill the men's sacks with food, as much as they can carry, and put every man's money in his sack's mouth. And put my cup, the silver cup, in the sack's mouth of the youngest, and his corn money. And he did according to the word that Joseph had spoken. As soon as the morning was light, the men were sent away, they and their asses.*
>
> Genesis 44:1–3

After the brothers had eaten and made merry with Joseph, he dismissed them, gave them the grain that they wanted, and sent them away. But before they left Egypt, Joseph told his steward, "Put my silver cup, in the sack of the youngest, and then put the sack at the top of the stack." This was similar to what Joseph did the first time his brothers came to Egypt.

Not long after they departed, Joseph sent the steward after them and he accused them of stealing the silver cup that Joseph drank from. Joseph had experienced firsthand the cruelty of his brothers. Here, he tested their loyalty to Benjamin to see if their hearts had changed.

Put to the Test

And *when they were gone out of the city*, and *not* yet *far off,* *Joseph said unto his steward, Up, follow after the men; and when thou dost overtake them, say unto them, Wherefore have ye rewarded evil for good?* Is *not this* it *in which my lord drinketh, and whereby indeed he divineth? ye have done evil in so doing. And he overtook them, and he spake unto them these same words.*

Genesis 44:4–6

Joseph had already been an instrument of God to bring his brothers to their senses and repentance (Gen. 42:21–24), but the job wasn't complete. It's not recorded in Scripture whether or not Joseph had shared with this steward who these men were. I wonder what he was thinking about all of this, knowing that he was the one who put the cup and the money in their sacks.

And they said unto him, Wherefore saith my lord these words? God forbid that thy servants should do according to this thing: Behold, the money, which we found in our sacks' mouths, we brought again unto thee out of the land of Canaan: how then should we steal out of thy lord's house silver or gold? With whomsoever of thy servants it be found, both let him die, and we also will be my lord's bondmen. And he said, Now also let it be according unto

your words: he with whom it is found shall be my servant;
and ye shall be blameless.

Genesis 44:7–10

I suspect Joseph's brothers had quite the conversation after leaving Joseph's house. They were probably feeling like everything worked out just fine and they had escaped the retribution they so feared (Gen. 42:21–22). But as Proverbs 13:12 says, *"Hope deferred maketh the heart sick."* Their hearts were about to be devastated.

This same steward who told these men that he was the one who put the money in their sacks the previous time and encouraged them not to fear was now accusing them of stealing his master's cup. This was a similar scenario. You would think that one of them would have figured it out, but the brothers made their third stupid oath in three chapters (Gen. 42:37 and 43:9). Their words didn't seem to mean very much to them. Anyone who would do the terrible things they had done throughout their lives would lie to save their own skin. But it turns out their rash oath suited Joseph's purposes perfectly.

Then they speedily took down every man his sack to the
ground, and opened every man his sack. And he searched,
and began at the eldest, and left at the youngest: and the cup
was found in Benjamin's sack. Then they rent their clothes,
and laded every man his ass, and returned to the city.

Genesis 44:11–13

Chapter 12

Humble Yourself Before God

And Judah and his brethren came to Joseph's house; for he was *yet there: and they fell before him on the ground. And Joseph said unto them, What deed* is *this that ye have done? wot ye not that such a man as I can certainly divine? And Judah said, What shall we say unto my lord? what shall we speak? or how shall we clear ourselves? God hath found out the iniquity of thy servants: behold, we* are *my lord's servants, both we, and* he *also with whom the cup is found.*

Genesis 44:14–16

Judah had no excuse. There was no way to justify himself. He said, *"God hath found out the iniquity of thy servants."* This was more than just bowing down to Joseph because he was in a position of authority. Now, the brothers were beginning to bow their knees to God. They were reaping what they'd sown (Gal. 6:7).

The sins they had committed were coming back to haunt them. These were wicked men who were living lawless lives.

They were defying God and everybody else. And now, they had finally realized that *the wages of sin is death* (Rom. 6:23).

I believe this is what God intended. This is the reason Joseph did all of these things to his brothers. It wasn't revenge. It was to break their self-will—their rebellion toward God— and bring them to a place of repentance.

> *And he said, God forbid that I should do so:* but *the man in whose hand the cup is found, he shall be my servant; and as for you, get you up in peace unto your father. Then Judah came near unto him, and said, Oh my lord, let thy servant, I pray thee, speak a word in my lord's ears, and let not thine anger burn against thy servant: for thou art even as Pharaoh. My lord asked his servants, saying, Have ye a father, or a brother? And we said unto my lord, We have a father, an old man, and a child of his old age, a little one; and his brother is dead, and he alone is left of his mother, and his father loveth him.*
>
> Genesis 44:17–20

Judah talks about when the brothers went back to Jacob and told him they couldn't buy more grain from Egypt unless they brought Benjamin with them. He said they couldn't get Jacob to agree to those conditions because he had already lost Joseph and he was afraid he'd lose Benjamin. Finally, when they just got so hungry, the brothers promised they would bring Benjamin back.

From the brothers' perspective, the information about Joseph's supposed death wasn't pertinent to the situation at hand. But Judah's confession about their treatment of him was at the core of their guilt, and they knew that it was why all these terrible things were happening to them.

This shows that none of us actually get by with sin (Num. 32:23). It weighs on us all through this life until confessed and repented of (1 John 1:9), and if we don't deal with it in this life, we will spend eternity dealing with the consequences (Rom. 6:23).

Change of Heart

Now therefore when I come to thy servant my father, and the lad be not with us; seeing that his life is bound up in the lad's life; It shall come to pass, when he seeth that the lad is not with us, that he will die: and thy servants shall bring down the gray hairs of thy servant our father with sorrow to the grave. For thy servant became surety for the lad unto my father, saying, If I bring him not unto thee, then I shall bear the blame to my father for ever. Now therefore, I pray thee, let thy servant abide instead of the lad a bondman to my lord; and let the lad go up with his brethren. For how shall I go up to my father, and the lad be not with me? lest peradventure I see the evil that shall come on my father.

Genesis 44:30–34

Remember, these brothers sold Joseph into slavery (Gen. 37:27–28). They took Joseph's coat of many colors, killed an animal, put blood all over the coat, and brought it back to their father (Gen. 37:31–32). And Jacob immediately jumped to the conclusion that some animal had killed Joseph and that his son was dead (Gen. 37:33–34). They lied to their father, and Jacob began to grieve (Gen. 37:34–35). They rose up to comfort him, but he would not be comforted. Jacob basically said, "I am going to my grave grieving for Joseph."

For twenty-two years, they had willingly let Jacob suffer grief and sorrow. They promoted themselves by getting rid of their problem. They got rid of their younger brother and even made some money at his expense (Gen. 37:26–27). They were willing to see their father live in grief all that time. You talk about being hardhearted!

If there had been any compassion at all in these men, they would've told Jacob the truth because they would've been brokenhearted to see their father suffering that way. But they just let it happen. Now that Benjamin was going to be taken away, they knew it would kill Jacob because his heart was wrapped up in the life of his son (Gen. 44:30).

Judah essentially said, "Take me as a slave, and let all of the others go back" (v. 33). These men had been so willing to hurt their father and see him grieve. They were willing to kill Joseph but instead sold him into slavery. It didn't appear they had had any remorse or grief about it. They hadn't told the truth for years. But finally, Judah came to the end of himself and was willing to become a slave. He and his brothers had a total change of heart from the treatment they had given Joseph and Jacob twenty-two years before.

Judah had finally come to a place where he was willing to sacrifice his life for the sake of his brothers and, specifically, for the sake of his father. After lying for twenty-two years about this whole situation, he was finally willing to come clean. Judah was finally willing to bear some responsibility.

I believe that's what all Joseph's dreams were about. It wasn't just about the brothers bowing their knees to Joseph. It was about bringing them to a place where they humbled themselves. They were actually bowing before God. These men had been resisting God. They had been shaking their fists in the face of God by the way they had been living. And God used Joseph to bring them to the end of themselves.

Moment of Truth

Then Joseph could not refrain himself before all them that stood by him; and he cried, Cause every man to go out from me. And there stood no man with him, while Joseph made himself known unto his brethren. And he wept aloud: and the Egyptians and the house of Pharaoh heard.

And Joseph said unto his brethren, I am Joseph; doth my father yet live? And his brethren could not answer him; for they were troubled at his presence.

Genesis 45:1–3

That is just amazing. These brothers didn't have a clue that Joseph was the one they had been dealing with the whole time. When he said, "I am Joseph," it says his brothers were troubled. You talk about an understatement.

The Bible sometimes grossly understates things, like when God created the heavens and the earth (Gen. 1:1). He saw the light and the Scripture says, *"that* it was *good"* (Gen. 1:4). It was awesome the way that God created everything, but we can't begin to know what it was like with our little peanut brains. So, the Bible just says, *"it was good."* It was just perfect.

I can only imagine what these brothers must have thought when they finally realized the man who accused them of being spies, locked up Simeon, threatened to take all of them as slaves, and then threatened to take Benjamin as a slave, was really Joseph all along. All of a sudden, every piece of the puzzle began to fit together.

When the brothers realized that Joseph was the one they were dealing with, it must have shocked them. Fear must have come upon them because they knew they deserved whatever Joseph gave them. If Joseph would've killed the ten of them on the spot, they would have deserved it. And I believe that realization began to sink in for the brothers.

And Joseph said unto his brethren, Come near to me, I pray you. And they came near. And he said, I am Joseph your brother, whom ye sold into Egypt. Now therefore be not grieved, nor angry with yourselves, that ye sold me hither: for God did send me before you to preserve life.

Genesis 45:4–5

This shows Joseph wasn't bitter. He didn't say, "I hope you've learned your lesson." He tried to console them and say, "Don't be angry with yourselves. Don't be disappointed. God used all of this. God sent me here to save lives." Joseph had a great attitude.

Haste ye, and go up to my father, and say unto him, Thus saith thy son Joseph, God hath made me lord of all Egypt: come down unto me, tarry not: And thou shalt dwell in the land of Goshen, and thou shalt be near unto me, thou, and thy children, and thy children's children, and thy flocks, and thy herds, and all that thou hast . . . Now thou art commanded, this do ye; take you wagons out of the land of Egypt for your little ones, and for your wives, and bring your father, and come. Also regard not your stuff; for the good of all the land of Egypt is yours.

Genesis 45:9–10 and 19–20

Joseph commanded them to return to Canaan with loaded wagons. He sent them all kinds of food and provisions, including wagons, horses, and animals. He told his brothers to get their father and bring him back to Egypt. Joseph also told them to get all their families, bring them back, and let the goodness of Egypt sustain them. Joseph told them they didn't have to bring their own household items because all the wealth of Egypt was theirs. They could have anything they wanted. That's awesome!

> *So he sent his brethren away, and they departed: and he said unto them, See that ye fall not out by the way.*
>
> Genesis 45:24

This is an old English way of saying, "Make sure you do what I told you to do." Because these men had lied and behaved badly for decades, Joseph wanted to make sure they followed through. It took a lot of faith on Joseph's part to turn these brothers free with all of these riches. But to their credit, they did go back to Canaan for their father and families, just as Joseph commanded.

A Joyous Reunion

> *And they went up out of Egypt, and came into the land of Canaan unto Jacob their father, And told him, saying, Joseph is yet alive, and he is governor over all the land*

*of Egypt. And Jacob's heart fainted, for he believed them
not. And they told him all the words of Joseph, which he
had said unto them: and when he saw the wagons which
Joseph had sent to carry him, the spirit of Jacob their
father revived: And Israel said, It is enough; Joseph my
son is yet alive: I will go and see him before I die.*

Genesis 45:25–28

What must Jacob have thought when he saw all the wagons, asses, and provisions that Joseph sent? Even before he
heard their story, he must have known something wonderful
had happened. I can only imagine what Jacob thought when
he found out Joseph was still alive after twenty-two years of
thinking that he was dead. And not only was he alive, but
Joseph was the second-most powerful man on the planet.

This could have been very hard for all the brothers, as well
as Jacob. What kind of justification could they have offered for
the deeds they had done? How would they have felt as their
father realized the grief he had felt every day for the last twenty-two years was wasted time and the result of their lies? This
could have made an irreparable breach in Jacob's relationship
with the sons who deceived him, but the joy of hearing Joseph
was still alive overwhelmed Jacob's anger, and he prepared
himself to see his son again.

*And Joseph made ready his chariot, and went up to meet
Israel his father, to Goshen, and presented himself unto*

him; and he fell on his neck, and wept on his neck a good while. And Israel said unto Joseph, Now let me die, since I have seen thy face, because thou art yet alive.

Genesis 46:29–30

How many times during Joseph's twenty-two years in Egypt did he long to see his father again? He had served as a slave and was unjustly cast into prison, holding on to the dreams God had given him. Joseph's second dream actually showed that his brothers *and* father all bowed to him (Gen. 37:9), so he certainly believed they would see each other again. But remember, Jacob had spent all that time believing his son was dead.

When Joseph finally met Jacob, they embraced for a long period of time, crying over each other. They were finally reunited.

And Joseph said unto his brethren, and unto his father's house, I will go up, and shew Pharaoh, and say unto him, My brethren, and my father's house, which were in the land of Canaan, are come unto me; And the men are shepherds, for their trade hath been to feed cattle; and they have brought their flocks, and their herds, and all that they have. . . . And Pharaoh spake unto Joseph, saying, Thy father and thy brethren are come unto thee: The land of Egypt is before thee; in the best of the land make thy father and brethren to dwell; in the land of Goshen let

them dwell: and if thou knowest any *men of activity*
among them, then make them rulers over my cattle.

Genesis 46:31–32 and 47:5–6

Joseph presented his family, and Pharaoh told them to go
to the land of Goshen. It's possible that over the nine years
Joseph and Pharaoh had known each other, Joseph related
what happened to him by his brothers, but Pharaoh doesn't
show any disrespect to them.

Secular history doesn't recognize this land of Goshen, but
Genesis 47:11 uses the phrase *"land of Rameses"* interchange-
ably with it. The "land of Rameses" is actually well established
in secular history. Also, Exodus 1:11 says the Israelites *"built*
for Pharaoh treasure cities, Pithom and Raamses," which are also
well known. So, this land of Goshen was in the eastern part of
Egypt, east of the Nile. Pharaoh described it as the best of the
land of Egypt (Gen. 47:6), which certainly suited Jacob's herds
and allowed him to continue to prosper.

Giving a Blessing

And Israel beheld Joseph's sons, and said, Who are these?
And Joseph said unto his father, They are *my sons, whom*
God hath given me in this place. *And he said, Bring*
them, I pray thee, unto me, and I will bless them. . . .
And Joseph took them both, Ephraim in his right hand

183

toward Israel's left hand, and Manasseh in his left hand
toward Israel's right hand, and brought them *near unto*
him. And Israel stretched out his right hand, and laid it
upon Ephraim's head, who was *the younger, and his left*
hand upon Manasseh's head, guiding his hands wittingly;
for Manasseh was *the firstborn.*

Genesis 48:8–9 and 13–14

Joseph brought in his two sons, Manasseh and Ephraim, to
Jacob for a blessing. and Joseph specifically guided the children
toward Jacob because the right hand held the greater blessing.
But Jacob held up his left hand to place upon the firstborn's head
and his right hand upon the second. Joseph tried to move them.

And when Joseph saw that his father laid his right hand
upon the head of Ephraim, it displeased him: and he held
up his father's hand, to remove it from Ephraim's head
unto Manasseh's head. And Joseph said unto his father, Not
so, my father: for this is *the firstborn; put thy right hand*
upon his head. And his father refused, and said, I know
it, *my son, I know* it: *he also shall become a people, and*
he also shall be great: but truly his younger brother shall
be greater than he, and his seed shall become a multitude
of nations. And he blessed them that day, saying, In thee
shall Israel bless, saying, God make thee as Ephraim and
as Manasseh: and he set Ephraim before Manasseh.

Genesis 48:17–20

It turned out that the youngest son got the blessing, and that became very important later in the history of the Jews. Ephraim became the dominant tribe even though Manasseh was the firstborn. Jacob had been the second born, yet he had prevailed over Esau (Gen. 25:25–26). He was prophesying the same thing over Ephraim.

When Jacob was dying, he called all of his sons in and blessed them (Gen. 49:1–27). Jacob died (Gen. 49:33), and Joseph fell upon his father's face and wept (Gen. 50:1). Notice how the Scripture points out that Joseph was the one who showed this open affection at Jacob's death. It's possible that the other children did too. But it's also possible that the ten brothers' lie about Joseph's death had strained their relationship with their father, and therefore, they didn't have the same affection for him. Their actions would certainly indicate that.

After Jacob died, they took him back to Israel and buried him in the sepulcher of Abraham and Isaac (Gen. 50:7–13). Afterward, Joseph and his brothers returned to Egypt. Now that the famine had passed, and the children of Israel had survived, what was to be served by Joseph and his family returning to Egypt?

First, Joseph's life and identity were all in Egypt. He had spent more time living there than in Canaan, and he was second in command to Pharaoh. Also, Joseph's brothers and their families were all flourishing in Egypt, since Goshen was the best of the land (Gen. 47:6). Regardless, the Lord had prophesied they wouldn't permanently leave Egypt and return to Canaan until the four hundred years of Genesis 15:13 were over.

Offering Assurance

And when Joseph's brethren saw that their father was dead, they said, Joseph will peradventure hate us, and will certainly requite us all the evil which we did unto him.

Genesis 50:15

After Jacob finally died, Joseph's brothers were afraid he was going to take vengeance on them (Gen. 50:15–17). They must have thought the only reason he was treating them nicely was because Jacob was still alive.

It certainly wasn't Joseph's fault that his brothers felt this way. Joseph had already told them he didn't blame them. He considered it God who had sent him to Egypt to preserve life (Gen. 45:3–6). It was his brothers' own consciences that brought this fear (John 8:9).

Likewise, it is not the Lord who condemns us (Rom. 8:1) but our own consciences (Rom. 2:15 and 1 John 3:19–21). We have to purge our consciences from dead works (Heb. 9:14) before we can freely serve the living God.

And they sent a messenger unto Joseph, saying, Thy father did command before he died, saying, So shall ye say unto Joseph, Forgive, I pray thee now, the trespass of thy brethren, and their sin; for they did unto thee evil: and now, we pray thee, forgive the trespass of the servants of the God of thy father. And Joseph wept when they spake unto him. And his brethren also went and fell down before his face; and they said, Behold, we be thy servants.

Genesis 50:16–18

This was a lie motivated by the brothers' lack of faith in Joseph, and it broke his heart that his brothers didn't believe him. They didn't actually believe he had forgiven and loved them. Likewise, it grieves the Spirit of God when we don't receive the complete freedom from condemnation that He has provided for us. Sure, Joseph's brothers didn't deserve his kindness, just like we don't deserve God's goodness. But Joseph gave it, just as God has given us His unconditional love through Jesus.

His brothers also fell before his face for the fifth and final time. They still were feeling the condemnation and the guilt of what they had done to Joseph, and because of it, they were willing to make themselves slaves for the rest of their lives. Joseph didn't want his brothers to be his slaves; he wanted them to receive his forgiveness and for them to be a family again. Likewise, Jesus elevated us from slaves to children and heirs of God (Gal. 4:7).

> *And Joseph said unto them, Fear not: for* am *I in the place of God? But as for you, ye thought evil against me;* but *God meant it unto good, to bring to pass, as* it is *this day, to save much people alive. Now therefore fear ye not: I will nourish you, and your little ones. And he comforted them, and spake kindly unto them.*
>
> Genesis 50:19–21

Joseph said, "I've never held anything against you. I would never take vengeance on you. God sent me here for your sakes." Joseph had no animosity toward his brothers at all. He had totally forgiven them.

Joseph knew his place, and it wasn't to occupy the rightful place that only God can fill. There is only one God, and we are not Him. We would all do well to remember that. At any time, he could have thrown his brothers in prison or had them killed, but he didn't do that. Joseph didn't let his power and influence go to his head.

Joseph was seventeen years old when his brothers sold him into slavery and thirty when he first stood before Pharaoh. He served as the second-most powerful man in Egypt through seven years of plenty and seven years of drought. He was married, raised a family, reconciled with his brothers, reunited with his father, and died at 110 years old, living long enough to see his great-great-grandchildren.

Overall, Joseph's life was exceedingly blessed. Praise God that he didn't falter in his faith during those thirteen years of slavery and imprisonment. In the same way, while we may go through hard times (John 16:33), we have been promised victory, and we will reap it *"if we faint not"* (Gal. 6:9).

Conclusion

But as for you, ye thought evil against me; but *God meant it unto good, to bring to pass, as* it is *this day, to save much people alive.*

Genesis 50:20

This reminds me of Romans 8:28, where Paul wrote, "*And we know that all things work together for good to them that love God, to them who are the called according to* his *purpose.*" I think this may be one of the most important lessons we can learn from the life of Joseph.

That verse in Romans has been interpreted by many to mean that God does everything to you and makes it work together for good. That's not what it says. It doesn't say all things come from God. It just says God can work things together for good.

God did not preordain that Joseph become a slave, then a prisoner. I do believe that God moved the brothers to sell Joseph into slavery rather than kill him. Out of the options they had, it was the one that worked for their good, because it ended up preserving all of the children of Jacob and the people of Egypt. Joseph was an instrument of God to bring his brothers to the end of themselves and to repentance. He remained faithful.

That's an example of how God can work things together for good. And I believe that's what Joseph was saying to his brothers. What they meant for evil, God worked together for good because Joseph loved the Lord and was called according to His purpose.

I've had people do a lot of things to me with evil intentions. But because I loved God and operated in what He called me to do, He has worked those things together for good. I can look at the bad things that have happened to me, and they've worked together for good. God can use anything that happens to you and work it together for good, but you can't blame God for causing those things.

You shouldn't just submit to and embrace your problems because those things are sent to steal, kill, and destroy (John 10:10). You have to resist those things (James 4:7). It's only as you resist them and apply your faith that those things work together for good.

Another major takeaway from Joseph's life is how he depended on God to bring his dreams to pass. He didn't take matters into his own hands even when he became the ruler of Egypt and could have forced his brothers to bow down to him. That dependence on God is what true humility is, and it's rare.

Lack of humility and self-will is probably Satan's biggest inroad into our lives. It's because the Lord loves us so much that He hasn't promoted us to the level He promoted Joseph. He knows we would not be able to handle the attacks the devil would throw at us.

Joseph could have griped and complained about his situation. He could have compromised his morals and sinned against God, given the opportunity. He could have been bitter toward his brothers and punished them through unforgiveness. He could have just thought, *What's the use? Nobody even knows where I am. I'll never get out of this prison.* But Joseph didn't do any of those things.

He held on to the dreams God had given him and trusted that they would come to pass. Joseph trusted God and let Him work together all those things for good. Because he remembered his dreams and trusted the Lord, his father and brothers benefitted, Egypt benefitted, and God got all the glory. Amen!

Further Study

If you enjoyed this book and would like to learn more about some of the things I've shared, I suggest my teachings:

- *How to Find, Follow, and Fulfill God's Will*

- *The Power of Imagination*

- *Ten Godly Leadership Essentials*

- *Excellence: How to Pursue an Excellent Spirit*

- *Lessons from David*

- *Lessons from Elijah*

- *More Grace, More Favor*

These teachings are available for free at **awmi.net**, or they can be purchased at **awmi.net/store**.

Receive Jesus as Your Savior

Choosing to receive Jesus Christ as your Lord and Savior is the most important decision you'll ever make!

God's Word promises, *"That if thou shalt confess with thy mouth the Lord Jesus, and shalt believe in thine heart that God hath raised him from the dead, thou shalt be saved. For with the heart man believeth unto righteousness; and with the mouth confession is made unto salvation"* (Rom. 10:9–10). *"For whosoever shall call upon the name of the Lord shall be saved"* (Rom. 10:13). By His grace, God has already done everything to provide salvation. Your part is simply to believe and receive.

Pray out loud: "Jesus, I acknowledge that I've sinned and need to receive what you did for the forgiveness of my sins. I confess that You are my Lord and Savior. I believe in my heart that God raised You from the dead. By faith in Your Word, I receive salvation now. Thank You for saving me."

The very moment you commit your life to Jesus Christ, the truth of His Word instantly comes to pass in your spirit. Now that you're born again, there's a brand-new you!

Please contact us and let us know that you've prayed to receive Jesus as your Savior. We'd like to send you some free materials to help you on your new journey. Call our Helpline: **719-635-1111** (available 24 hours a day, seven days a week) to speak to a staff member who is here to help you understand and grow in your new relationship with the Lord.

Welcome to your new life!

Receive the Holy Spirit

As His child, your loving heavenly Father wants to give you the supernatural power you need to live a new life. *"For every one that asketh receiveth; and he that seeketh findeth; and to him that knocketh it shall be opened…how much more shall your heavenly Father give the Holy Spirit to them that ask him?"* (Luke 11:10–13).

All you have to do is ask, believe, and receive!

Pray this: "Father, I recognize my need for Your power to live a new life. Please fill me with Your Holy Spirit. By faith, I receive it right now. Thank You for baptizing me. Holy Spirit, You are welcome in my life."

Some syllables from a language you don't recognize will rise up from your heart to your mouth (1 Cor. 14:14). As you speak them out loud by faith, you're releasing God's power from within and building yourself up in the spirit (1 Cor. 14:4). You can do this whenever and wherever you like.

It doesn't really matter whether you felt anything or not when you prayed to receive the Lord and His Spirit. If you believed in your heart that you received, then God's Word promises you did. *"Therefore I say unto you, What things soever ye desire, when ye pray, believe that ye receive* them, *and ye shall have* them" (Mark 11:24). God always honors His Word—believe it!

We would like to rejoice with you, pray with you, and answer any questions to help you understand more fully what has taken place in your life!

Please contact us to let us know that you've prayed to be filled with the Holy Spirit and to request the book *The New You & the Holy Spirit*. This book will explain in more detail about the benefits of being filled with the Holy Spirit and speaking in tongues. Call our Helpline: **719-635-1111** (available 24 hours a day, seven days a week).

Call for Prayer

If you need prayer for any reason, you can call our Helpline, 24 hours a day, seven days a week at **719-635-1111**. A trained prayer minister will answer your call and pray with you.

Every day, we receive testimonies of healings and other miracles from our Helpline, and we are ministering God's nearly-too-good-to-be-true message of the Gospel to more people than ever. So, I encourage you to call today!

Endnotes

1   T.E. Lawrence, *Seven Pillars of Wisdom*: A Triumph, Delhi: Oxford University Press, 1940, 23, accessed March 7, 2023, https://archive.org/details/in.ernet.dli.2015.462697/page/n21/mode/2up.

2   "WHO Coronavirus (COVID-19) Dashboard," World Health Organization, accessed May 9, 2023, https://covid19.who.int/.

3   "U.S. and World Population Clock," United States Census Bureau, accessed May 9, 2023, https://www.census.gov/popclock/.

4   "Influenza: 1918 Pandemic," Centers for Disease Control and Prevention, accessed May 1, 2023, https://www.cdc.gov/flu/pandemic-resources/1918-pandemic-h1n1.html.

5   "Historical Estimates of World Population," United States Census Bureau, accessed May 9, 2023, https://www.census.gov/data/tables/time-series/demo/international-programs/historical-est-worldpop.html.

6   *Strong's Definitions*, s.v. "מְנַשֶּׁה" ("mᵊnaššê"), accessed May 10, 2023, https://www.blueletterbible.org/lexicon/h4519/kjv/wlc/0-1/.

7   *Strong's Definitions*, s.v. "אֶפְרַיִם" ("eᵽrayim"), accessed May 10, 2023, https://www.blueletterbible.org/lexicon/h669/kjv/wlc/0-1/.

ABOUT THE AUTHOR

Andrew Wommack's life was forever changed the moment he encountered the supernatural love of God on March 23, 1968. As a renowned Bible teacher and author, Andrew has made it his mission to change the way the world sees God.

Andrew's vision is to go as far and deep with the Gospel as possible. His message goes far through the Gospel Truth television program, which is available to over half the world's population. The message goes deep through discipleship at Charis Bible College, headquartered in Woodland Park, Colorado. Founded in 1994, Charis has campuses across the United States and around the globe.

Andrew also has an extensive library of teaching materials in print, audio, and video. More than 200,000 hours of free teachings can be accessed at **awmi.net**.

Contact Information

Andrew Wommack Ministries, Inc.

P.O. Box 3333

Colorado Springs, CO 80934-3333

info@awmi.net

awmi.net

Helpline: 719-635-1111 (available 24/7)

Charis Bible College

info@charisbiblecollege.org

844-360-9577

CharisBibleCollege.org

For a complete list of our offices, visit **awmi.net/contact-us**.

Connect with us on social media.